**West Federal Taxation**

TAX RETURN
PREPARATION
with TurboTax® Personal Tax Software

Jerrold J. Stern, Indiana University

Intuit®, San Diego, California

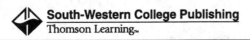
South-Western College Publishing
Thomson Learning™

Australia • Canada • Mexico • Singapore • Spain • United Kingdom • United States

Tax Return Preparation with TurboTax® for Windows, Personal Tax Software, Contains 1999 Tax Forms, by Jerrold J. Stern and Intuit®

Vice President/ Team Director: Dave Shaut
Sponsoring Editor: Scott D. Person
Developmental Editor: Carol Bennett
Production Editor: Barbara Fuller Jacobsen
Media Production Editor: Lora Craver
Marketing Manager: Jennifer Codner
Manufacturing Coordinator: Doug Wilke
Printer: Mazer

Printed in the United States of America
  2 3 4 5 03 02 01 00

For more information contact South-Western College Publishing, 5101 Madison Road, Cincinnati, Ohio, 45227 or find us on the Internet at http://www.swcollege.com

For permission to use material from this text or product, contact us by
- telephone: 1-800-730-2214
- fax: 1-800-730-2215
- Web: http://www.thomsonrights.com

ISBN 0-324-01470-8 (packaged manual and CD-ROM)

This book is printed on acid-free paper.

PREFACE

West's Federal Taxation Tax Return Preparation with TurboTax manual is designed to support the use of TurboTax software in the classroom. TurboTax is a widely used tax return preparation software package. Most tax professors are quick to point to the advantages of having students complete tax returns; some also point out the related disadvantages. Two of these are: (1) time consuming redundancy that occurs when students transfer data between tax forms, and (2) having an adequate supply of tax forms with related instructions. TurboTax software offers solutions to both of these problems.

At the option of the user, TurboTax can be very tax form oriented. The student may examine forms and related worksheets (displayed on screen) and complete each by entering data. An advantage with electronic tax return preparation is that the student does not have to do excessive computations or copy information from one form to another. Each available tax form displays on the screen virtually identically to official IRS forms. Second, several TurboTax worksheets are interactive: the worksheet leads the user through a complicated area of the tax law by asking relevant questions. Third, with internet access to the IRS web site (www.irs.ustreas.gov) the student has online access to IRS forms and official IRS instructions. The TurboTax help system is structured in such a manner that the user learns to identify tax problems, research the answer, and report data correctly on tax forms.

This version of TurboTax is limited to individual tax returns. Other versions of TurboTax, discussed briefly in Chapter 2, support the preparation of Partnership returns (Form 1065) and Corporation returns (Forms 1120 and 1120S). By using TurboTax to prepare individual tax returns, students can learn much about tax law, tax return preparation, and current tax technology.

You can use TurboTax to prepare returns in either of two ways: (1) EasyStep® Interview or, (2) Forms Method. The EasyStep Interview is designed as a guided tour and is best for a student's first attempt at tax preparation. Forms Method is faster, but requires detailed knowledge of tax forms. This manual discusses both methods in detail.

Each year, TurboTax is updated for users. New features for tax year 1999 include:

1. **Progress Bar** - The Progress Bar makes it easy to find specific topics and to move to different parts of the tax return. It is located across the top of the TurboTax screen, below the menu bar. Each button on the Progress Bar addresses a different section of the tax return.

2. **Show Tax Form/Hide Tax Form** - When information is entered, you have the option of seeing the tax form that you are working on in the lower part of the EasyStep screen. This allows you to see where the information is recorded on each tax form.

The second half of the 1990's is an exciting time for the development and application of technology to the practice of tax preparation. Several firms are developing career paths for tax accountants who specialize in tax technology. All tax students are expected to know how to use various types of technology before they begin their first day of professional employment. Electronic tax return preparation may be the very first assignment for a newly-hired accountant even if the accountant's responsibilities include a substantial amount of non-tax work. Learning to use TurboTax will help provide this skill set.

Electronic tax return preparation is not the only technology used by tax advisers. The ability to use electronic tax research services on CD-ROM and the World Wide Web is equally important, as is the use of e-mail to communicate with clients and other tax advisers. Another source of tax information includes online services (such as *Lexis*, Research Institute of America's (RIA) *Checkpoint*, and the Commerce Clearing House (CCH) Internet Tax Research NetWork). Without question, all tax advisers need to be able to use technology effectively.

For more information about Intuit Inc. products, including TurboTax, Quicken®, QuickBooks®, QuickenMortgage®, and ProSeries® refer to the brief discussion at the beginning of Chapter 2, Overview of TurboTax. For further details, see these Intuit Inc. sites on the World Wide Web at the following URLs:

http://www.turbotax.com

http://www.intuit.com

As a tax preparer, you must be familiar with information available on the Internet. The volume of information on the Web is overwhelming; the amount of useful information is impressive.

TURBOTAX® IN THE CLASSROOM

The primary focus of most tax courses is to give the student an understanding of how the tax system works and the basics of tax law. The tax return preparation process is considered a secondary topic that may in fact be passed over by some professors. However, the first tax job of many students will be to prepare some type of tax return. An understanding of the various tax forms helps the student understand how different areas of tax law are related.

In 1992, the Committee on Computer Applications of the American Taxation Association conducted a survey of tax accounting professors. The survey covered three areas:

1. Reasons for using computers in tax education
2. Software used by tax accounting professors
3. Courses using computer technology

While some of the study's findings are dated, it nonetheless reports major reasons for using or not using computers in tax education that are relevant today. The primary reasons for using computers in tax education as reported by tax accounting professors are that they:

1. Prepare student for real-world situations.
2. Increase emphasis on tax planning.

Others reasons for using computer technology are that it

3. Facilitates learning basic tax topics.
4. Keeps the tax course on the cutting edge of tax education.
5. Increases efficiency in teaching tax topics.

The primary reason that computers are not used in tax education is the lack of time available to cover necessary topics in the course. A second reason is the lack of software useful in teaching tax topics.

TurboTax software supports the use of computers in tax education in several ways. First, TurboTax follows the design of the paper tax forms. Thus, inputting tax data in TurboTax gives students the same learning experience as manually writing the data on a paper form. The software automatically carries forward the amounts to the correct line on Form 1040. As a result, students avoid the clerical task of carrying forward totals as instructed on the forms. Some argue that, without this task, students will tend to not read the forms closely. However, students will be able to see how the forms are related to each other. This is one way the software adds value to the tax learning process.

The purpose of this manual is to increase classroom efficiency. The time required to learn to use TurboTax is added to the student's time spent outside of class. The more time students spend learning tax concepts, rules, and computations, the better equipped they will be to face the many challenges of being a professional tax accountant.

In addition to tax preparation, the TurboTax What-if option is very useful as a tax planning aid. The user can compare the tax results under four alternatives using the **Tool Menu** option, **What-if**. TurboTax also supports tax computation using estimated 2000 rates and tax law. The combination of a forms orientation and the What-if option make TurboTax supportive of the primary reasons for using computers in tax education. Perhaps this is the reason a survey of tax professors found TurboTax to be the most used tax preparation software in tax accounting education.

An analysis of the users of computer technology in tax education indicates that the discriminating application between users and non-users is electronic tax research. Today's tax technology focus is on the ability to use advanced applications to eliminate procedural tasks. TurboTax aids both of these desired ends. To eliminate procedural tasks, TurboTax provides a user-friendly interactive interview, referred to as EasyStep Interview. This interview is a series of questions designed to guide the tax preparer through the return. As the student answers questions related to the taxpayer's transactions, TurboTax enters and calculates data on the appropriate tax forms. Totals are then electronically transferred from detailed tax forms (such as Schedule C which calculates net income or loss from self-employment) to summary forms (such as Form 1040). EasyStep Interview may be said to "take students by the hand and lead them through the tax return."

The TurboTax Help function, which is context sensitive, provides an electronic tax research perspective. Thus, when you move the cursor to a specific line and select Help, TurboTax displays the help options for that specific line. The availability of detailed IRS instructions and TurboTax tax aids, displayed on the screen almost instantly, allows tax students the opportunity to examine less complex areas of tax law that will not be covered in class. The Help function also provides the option of searching the Help topics using key words, similar to the method used by electronic tax research products, such as *Lexis* and *Checkpoint*. Thus, students have the opportunity to learn useful electronic tax research techniques. Lastly, students can access official IRS instructions via Help.

In summary, using TurboTax in a tax class has specific advantages over other tax preparation alternatives. The student will be able to view tax forms on screen and learn the organization of various forms without the clerical burdens of arithmetic, copying, and transferring data from a detail supporting form to Form 1040. Users have consistently indicated that TurboTax is easy to use and has a short learning curve. This manual is written in a style that is intended to be easy to read. For tax law support, students have both TurboTax tax aids and online IRS instructions available at the touch of a key. Even though this specific software may not be used by paid preparers, the aspiring tax professional is exposed to tax return preparation as it is done in the real world. The best way to understand the advantages and disadvantages of using tax return preparation software is to use it. Using TurboTax helps young tax advisors prepare for the professional world they are about to enter. Included in the manual are 30 tax problems to provide practice using TurboTax software.

TABLE OF CONTENTS

CHAPTER 1

INTRODUCTION

The 1990s has been a decade of automation. Technology is growing in importance in every aspect of business including accounting and taxation. In fact, today's tax advisors cannot practice without the use of tax technology. The term "tax technology" refers to the use of computer and related technology in tax practice and can be defined as the use of computers, software, printers, communication hardware, and storage devices in tax practice.

The core of tax technology is computerized tax return preparation and tax research (via CD-ROM or the World Wide Web). In the professional world, computers have been used to increase the efficiency of completing a tax return. This allows tax advisors to spend more time analyzing increasingly complicated tax laws.

In addition to tax preparation and tax research, other uses of tax technology are:

- the use of specialized tax planning software referred to as Tax Decision Support Software,
- tax planning,
- electronic filing,
- word processing and electronic mail, and
- the use of the Internet to access new and innovative sources of tax information.

The purpose of this manual is to support your use of TurboTax in preparing tax returns. The software that is included with this manual is "TurboTax for Windows, 1999 Edition" by Intuit Inc. The software is not a student version; in fact you may prepare your personal tax return with the software. This version of TurboTax provides you with all the forms and schedules that you are likely to need. This manual is designed to be used by students who aspire to be professional accountants, who have recently begun to learn tax law and who are not experts in using personal computers.

Before you begin using TurboTax, you should understand the big picture of tax return preparation. Accordingly, in the sections below, you will read about the tax return preparation process and take a brief look at tax return preparation software in general. If you cannot wait to begin using TurboTax, go directly to Chapter 2.

TAX RETURN PREPARATION PROCESS

Prior to filing a tax return, tax information must be gathered, summarized according to tax accounts, and entered on the appropriate tax form. Regardless of whether a tax return is prepared manually or with the aid of a computer, the steps to follow are similar. The general steps in filing a tax return are as follows:

- Gather and summarize tax data.
- Research tax return preparation questions.
- Enter tax data on the appropriate return and document the source of the data used.
- Review the tax return.
- File the tax return.

Gathering and Summarizing Tax Data

Typically, the most painful part of preparing an individual tax return is reviewing past transactions to gather the necessary information. The required effort depends upon the economic circumstances of the taxpayer involved and the method the taxpayer used to store transaction information and documentation (i.e., receipts, canceled checks, statements, etc.).

With business returns, the information normally is contained in a general ledger. Typically the information will be organized by account numbers and a trial balance will be available. If the information has been audited, the amounts are assumed to be correct for tax preparation purposes. If the data are unaudited, the information should be reviewed to identify possible errors. The review will normally require the detailed accounts be reviewed and some source documents examined to ensure the data are correct. Even though the purpose of the data review is to prepare a tax return, the professional standards of the accounting profession (as set forth in the American Institute of CPAs' (AICPA) Statement of Responsibilities in Tax Practice No. 3) requires that the tax return preparer "... not ignore the implications of information furnished and should make reasonable inquiries if the information appears to be incorrect, incomplete or inconsistent either on its face or on the basis of other facts ..."

If the information has been audited, an audited trial balance is the source of tax data. The job of a tax return preparer is to regroup the accounts to reflect the information needed for the tax return. Many software packages used in the audit process provide an optional account grouping that will automatically reorganize the accounts in a format suitable for tax reporting. This tax grouping must be coded at the time that the various accounts are set up in the auditing software. If audit software has not been used in the audit, the tax return preparer will have to regroup the accounts with a manual or electronic worksheet.

If the information has not been recorded or summarized, the tax return preparer will have to develop a chart of accounts that corresponds to the lines on the tax return, and enter the details of each transaction into the appropriate account. Many tax return preparers refer to this situation as the "shoe box" approach, so called because many taxpayers choose a shoe box to store their receipts, checks, and other documentation of yearly transactions. Use of a simple electronic worksheet, general ledger software, or trial balance software will lessen the pain and shorten the time required to prepare a return.

With the advent of the personal computer, many individuals are using financial management software to record cash receipts and disbursements in the same manner as general ledger accounting software packages. Tax return preparation software supports the direct interface of most financial management/accounting software. If supported, the financial data can be summarized with the accounting software and directly imported to the tax return preparation software. TurboTax supports direct interface with *Quicken®*, and *QuickBooks®* (using the **TaxLink** command) and other financial programs. Other financial management programs that use Tax Exchange Format (TXF) files are supported with the general interface command, **Import**, discussed in Chapter 4. In late 1993, Intuit Inc., the creator of *Quicken®*, purchased ChipSoft, Inc., the creator of TurboTax. Thus, there is a high level of integration between the two software programs. However, the general acceptability of TXF files means that tax preparation software will interface with a wide variety of general ledger/accounting software packages.

The normal order used in gathering information follows the organization of the tax return. First the taxpayer's name, address, and identifying numbers are recorded. Next, the income items are gathered and entered on the return. Then the deductions are identified. If available, the previous year's tax return should be reviewed in order to identify recurring transactions. If tax preparation software is used, the software carries over continuing items (such as names, income sources, depreciation schedules, etc.) to the next year. With TurboTax, the **Transfer from last year** command is used to copy relevant information from the prior year tax return to the current year tax return.

The importance of a continuing file of prior year's tax returns cannot be overstated. Information as to the previous year's income from various types of property can lead to discovery of gains or losses from the sale of such property. Similarly, sources of income from the previous year can be expected to continue into the current year. Thus, comparison of the current year's information with the previous year's is crucial to the tax return preparation process.

Data gathering is the first and frequently the most time consuming step. After data has been gathered, the taxability of the transactions must be determined. Often, tax return preparers will have to research various sources of tax law to determine how to report transactions on the tax return.

Researching Tax Return Preparation Questions

In recent years, the tax laws have become so complex that tax return preparers are reluctant to express opinions on the tax status of a transaction without referring to tax reference materials. The source of the tax reference depends upon the chosen tax return processing method. If tax preparation software is used, the software may provide an online tax reference indexed to the specific line on the tax form. The tax reference materials used by TurboTax are the TurboTax tax aids and plain-English explanations of what to enter for the selected tax form line. Professional versions of some tax preparation software, like Intuit Inc.'s ProSeries® program, interface directly with CD-ROM tax research materials such CCH's *ACCESS*, RIA's *OnPoint,* or online services such as CCH's *Internet Tax Research NetWork*. Of course, other online electronic services such as WestLaw or Lexis, as well as hard copies of tax research materials are also available.

The goal in researching return preparation questions is to determine the correct tax result of a **completed** transaction and the correct location on the tax return to report each transaction. Typically, a formal research report is not prepared, but a complete list of references, and a statement of research conclusion is required. In most cases, reference to a secondary source, such as a publishing company's editorial comments, is acceptable. If the amount of tax at risk is large, a formal tax research report, citing **primary sources** of tax law (e.g., Internal Revenue Code, Treasury Regulations, court cases, IRS rulings, etc.) should be prepared and kept on file in case there is an IRS audit. In some cases, your research will not result in an answer about which you have 100 percent confidence. This occurs when the correct answer must be deduced from related court cases, rulings, or regulations. In these situations, the research report should clearly set forth the logic that links the taxpayer's facts with primary sources of tax law and the conclusion reached by the researcher.

Techniques for documenting the results of tax research vary between firms. The overriding objective is for the tax researcher to provide a trail from the specific item in question to the tax research materials used. With electronic tax return preparation, electronic notes can be added to document the research performed and the results of that research. Memos to the taxpayer client file can also be created.

Documentation of tax return data

The preparer's declaration on tax returns states that the information contained therein is true, correct, and complete to the best of the preparer's knowledge and belief, "based on all information of which the preparer has any knowledge." The statement is understood to relate to all information provided by the client or third parties. Accordingly, the tax return preparer may be asked to produce documentation of the source of information used in return preparation. At the present time, the IRS expects documentation in paper form. Examples include copies of canceled checks, copies of Form 1099, copies of trial balances, copies of invoices for large expenditures, lists of records kept by taxpayer and their location, and copies of financial statements. If the return is prepared with tax preparation software, the tax return preparer will need to maintain a paper file with copies of all information provided in addition to the electronic file generated by the tax preparation software. If data are provided to the preparer in electronic form, a trial balance from a general ledger file for example, a copy of the electronic files should be kept by the preparer. While not tested in the courts, the acceptability of electronic files as evidence is so similar to that of microfilm, which is accepted by the Federal Rules of Evidence, that tax return preparers are able to record information electronically and do away with paper storage. However at the current time, tax return preparation software will be used to create a paper tax return and paper supporting documents will normally be stored in the same manner as if the returns were prepared manually.

One of the developing problems of the last half of the 1990's is the increasing use of Electronic Data Interchange (EDI) by most large companies and many smaller companies. With EDI, there is no paper trail. Tax auditors are uncomfortable in such an environment and they pass on their feelings to the tax preparer. An example is Revenue Procedure 98-25, 1998-11 IRB, in which the IRS requires that taxpayers "maintain and make available to the IRS upon request documentation of the business processes that: (1) create the retained records; (2) modify and maintain its records." etc. In this age of fast changing technology, does this mean that the taxpayer must keep old operating systems available that can read the files created four or more years ago? Imagine trying to read a 5.25 floppy disk formatted with DOS 2.1. Many PCs today simply cannot do it. Add the problems of the firm that has changed from DOS to UNIX or some other operating system and the problems multiply. When everyone created a paper trail, the format of the data was not a problem. With an EDI system in place, operating system and format problems float to the surface.

Welcome to the Information Age!

Reviewing the Return

The normal steps in the preparation of a tax return include a review of the return by someone other than the preparer. In the case of a preparer who works alone, that review is normally done on another day so that the data and return may be given a fresh look. In either case, the goal is to detect any errors or omissions. The use of tax return preparation software makes it possible to create an all electronic tax file. All notes from the taxpayer and all tax data may be recorded electronically, eliminating the need for a paper file. The IRS will accept an electronic record in support of a tax return if that is the way the initial transaction is filed. Scanning of paper documents for storage purposes has not yet been considered by the IRS. Thus, while the availability of electronic filing does allow a paperless tax return, some tax preparers still maintain a paper record of the taxpayer interview and refer to that paper in the review process prior to filing. At your option, TurboTax can also perform a review of the return. This is accomplished by clicking the Review tab after all data has been entered.

The tax profession has not fully addressed these complications. As noted, current practice is to require a paper record of the interview with the taxpayer. Also, as noted above, paper copies of all information provided should be kept. At this time, the full productivity gains available with electronic tax return preparation are not being realized. Most tax preparation software does provide an online internal check of the return. Generally, this checks for consistency in the data entered and for completeness of data entered. The TurboTax command for this procedure is named **Review**. Currently, the review of a computer prepared return is being conducted similarly to the review of a manually prepared tax return.

Filing the tax return (Delivery to the IRS)

Electronic filing availability has increased rapidly in the 1990s. Most taxpayers are eligible to file their Federal tax returns electronically. Some taxpayers may be precluded from filing electronically if the return contains certain atypical forms or requires certain types of supporting information. Most states allow State returns to be electronically filed as well. It is estimated that 20 million 1999 federal and state tax returns will be filed electronically.

TurboTax enables electronic filing of both Federal and State returns. The fee for electronically processing a Federal return is $9.95. For a State return, the fee is $4.95. TurboTax transmits the return via the Internet to the Intuit Inc. Electronic Filing Center using a secure Internet connection. The return is then converted to a standardized format and transferred to the IRS or State taxing authority. Most taxpayers must follow up electronic filing with a one-page paper tax form (Form 8453-OL) and, in some cases, attachments. The main reason for the paper form is to provide a signature to the IRS. Some taxpayers have been selected by the IRS to file their return 100 percent electronically and completely avoid paper filings. A small percentage of taxpayers have already received an official letter from the IRS giving them an *e-file* Customer Number (called an ECN); TurboTax prompts taxpayers to enter their ECN if they have one. The IRS promises a faster turnaround time for taxpayers expecting a refund, if they file their return electronically.

ELECTRONIC TAX RETURN PREPARATION

The advantages of electronic tax return preparation are listed in an AICPA Tax Division's document, *Automation of the Tax Practice of the '90s*. The major advantages of automation are:

1. Perform work more quickly.
2. Produce higher quality work in the same amount of time.
3. Consider more alternatives in the same amount of time.
4. Produce a better looking work product.

The most common form of processing tax returns with computers is in-house processing. In-house processing refers to the use of software and hardware owned by the preparer. None of the tax data leaves the preparer's location. Typically the preparer will purchase professional tax preparation software from a software developer, such as Intuit Inc., the developers of ProSeries (professional version) and TurboTax (personal version). The entire tax return process, from input of data to printing of the final return is done in-house, i.e., on the preparer's premises.

One major concern with in-house electronic tax return preparation is that the preparer must identify the best preparation software for the firm and purchase that software on an annual basis. The time required to learn a new software product is costly. Thus, if the same software is used annually, the required training cost is minimized.

The cost of hardware for an in-house system is easily justified. In the early days of computer tax preparation, the cost of hardware was a constraint to in-house processing. However, the cost of computer processing has come down greatly.

Hardware and System Requirements

With the advances in personal computers and laser printers, many preparers are finding that the PC provides all the computer power necessary to process tax returns. Processing tax returns does require significant computations and is therefore impacted by the type of processor used in the personal computer. Also, because of the number of MS-DOS personal computers still in use, most software is written to use the Microsoft Windows 95 or 98 operating system. (The TurboTax for Windows version is included with this manual.) Thus, an IBM PC or compatible personal computer is required for most tax return preparation software. However, if the number of Apple Macintosh PCs increases, the number of software packages written for the Macintosh will also increase. (TurboTax is available in a Macintosh version called MacInTax®.)

Tax software is computationally orientated, thus, the speed of its operation can be improved with a fast microprocessor such as Intel's Pentium series microprocessors which include a math coprocessor to speed computations. (A math coprocessor is not required with TurboTax.) If the internet is to be used, the PC must be equipped with communication capability (via modem or LAN).

Most tax return preparation software has a graphical orientation, called a "graphical user interface," or GUI. With a GUI, the user sees graphical images such as tax return forms and icons along with text and data, rather than text and data alone. When Microsoft Windows is used, the software displays the tax return as it will be printed.

Laser jet or ink jet printers can be used with professional tax return preparation software. Because of various differences between printers, software known as "printer drivers," must be available for your specific printer. All tax return preparation software supports the leading brands of printers. It is best to check the software manual or check with the vendor before purchasing a printer to insure that you will not have compatibility problems, especially if a recognized market leader is not purchased. TurboTax supports a wide range of printers.

Selecting a Software Package

The first step in determining the specific software package to use is to analyze the type of returns that you expect to prepare. This can be a time consuming process, especially if it must be done manually. The AICPA Tax Division publication, *Automation of the Tax Practice of the 90s,* provides excellent worksheets to aid in manually preparing this analysis. Once the analysis is completed, software products can be sorted into those that support the forms you will require. Another deciding factor in the selection of specific software will be whether or not the software will prepare the state tax returns that are needed by the preparer. If the state return must be prepared manually, productivity may be lost.

Another factor is the extent to which electronic tax research is performed. CCH's *Internet Tax Research NetWork* and RIA's *Checkpoint* are currently the most comprehensive web-based tax research products. Both have built-in tax return preparation software components. Thus, some firms face a joint decision. They have to choose the package of software products that best suits their needs.

Current information regarding costs, capabilities, and availability is published in the September edition of the *Journal of Accountancy* and the October editions of the *Journal of Taxation* and *Taxation For Accountants*. In addition, reviews of software products are published by computer magazines such as *InfoWorld, PC World,* and *PC Magazine.* Various accounting newsletters also publish lists of software and number of users. Searching the web can yield a variety of sources that provide more reviews.

The primary factors to consider in choosing tax preparation software are:

- Are the needed state tax returns supported?
- Are most forms supported by the software?
- Is the cost reasonable?
- Are updates prepared each year, on a timely basis?
- Does the software developer provide support services?
- Does the software provide an interface with accounting software?
- Does the software provide on-line help?
- Is the software part of a larger package of software products?

As a general guideline, it is always better to try it before you buy it. Most software vendors provide low cost demonstration versions to a preparer so they can evaluate the product. It is important that the preparer, not a vendor, select the software that is best for the returns to be prepared.

Software Media

One of the newer features of tax preparation software is a change in the software media. Software is commonly distributed on high density disks (3.5 inch, 1.4MB disk, or CD-ROM). CD-ROM disks generally provide space for 650 megabytes or more of data. Intuit Inc. offers most their products on CD-ROM and many can be downloaded from their web site. A web version of *OnPoint*, called *Checkpoint*, became available in 1997. The extra storage capacity on CD-ROMs enables storage of multimedia materials - such as video and audio clips that provide tax and financial advice.

CHAPTER 2

OVERVIEW OF TURBOTAX®

Intuit Inc. develops user-friendly business and accounting software and related products for three unique markets - individuals, businesses, and professional accountants. *TurboTax* is used for preparing personal tax returns (Form 1040) and *TurboTax for Business* prepares returns for corporations (Form 1120), S corporations (Form 1120S), partnerships and most limited liability companies (Form 1065). *TurboTax Home & Business* prepares sole proprietorship tax forms (Form 1040 and related schedules). *ProSeries* is designed for use by professional tax accountants. All *TurboTax* software operates on IBM PCs and compatibles. *MacInTax* is the Macintosh version of *TurboTax*. Users can acquire Intuit Inc. software on CD-ROM. State products are also available for purchase on 3.5" disk. Products may also be downloaded from the Intuit Inc. web site (www.turbotax.com).

Other Intuit Inc. products include Quicken and QuickBooks. These packages perform a wide variety of personal and small business finance and accounting functions including check-writing, checking account analysis, budgeting, payroll, and financial statement preparation. Users can electronically copy financial information from this software directly into Intuit Inc. tax software for tax return preparation. Intuit's QuickenMortgage® on the web provides daily mortgage rates, enables homebuyers to obtain pre-approval for a mortgage loan, and facilitates a number of home purchase and financing analyses (such as "Rent vs. Buy" and "Rates vs. Points").

To find out more about these and additional Intuit Inc. products, visit the Intuit Inc. web site at

http://www.intuit.com

READ THIS BEFORE YOU START

As mentioned before, TurboTax is designed to be used by taxpayers who prepare their own return and not by professional tax return preparers. It is easy to use and includes a variety of sophisticated tools to help the user. Pull-down menus operate in a manner consistent with popular business software; most tax students who use Windows based software find the menus both familiar and useful.

TurboTax provides two methods of tax form preparation - EasyStep Interview and Forms Method. The EasyStep Interview is a comprehensive interactive interview that leads the user through the tax return preparation. Answers to interview questions help TurboTax decide which tax forms and tax rules are relevant to you. You are only asked questions that are relevant to your personal tax situation. TurboTax automatically places your responses on the appropriate tax forms. This approach speeds the tax return preparation process considerably. You will be able to see where TurboTax is entering your data because the form being used is displayed in the lower portion of the screen. TurboTax automatically makes all necessary computations. One major difference between TurboTax and spreadsheet software like Lotus and Excel is that you will not be able to see the formulas TurboTax uses to make tax calculations.

In Forms Method, you select the forms you want to complete and enter the required information. Knowledge of tax return preparation is necessary to accurately use Forms Method. You can access Forms Method directly by clicking on Forms in the menu bar in the upper left-hand corner of the screen. Alternatively, you can access the form associated with the interview questions currently on your screen by clicking on the Show Tax Form button located at the bottom of the screen. A portion of the form will appear in a window at the bottom of the screen. Click on the Go to Forms ... button located in the form window. The form will then fill the entire screen. From there, you can move down the form to the line where your transaction is reported and go to the appropriate supporting statement by double clicking on that line. To return to EasyStep Interview, simply click on the Back to Interview button in the upper right-hand corner of the screen. These methods are discussed more fully in the following chapters.

Data Source is one of the help features. While using Forms Method, you can move the cursor to any field. Then, pressing the **right** button on your mouse will display a menu of which one option is **Data Source**. Selecting **Data Source** displays the source of any calculated amounts. TurboTax uses the term "calculated amounts" to refer to any data item that is either transferred from another location in TurboTax or is the result of a calculation on the current form. Also, if the field is a calculated amount, a magnifying glass icon is displayed adjacent to the field. Clicking on the icon moves you to the form that is the source of the amount. Thus, by using **Data Source** you can determine how the forms are interconnected, and by clicking on the magnifying glass icon, you can see those forms. Doing so will help you better understand the tax forms and how they are linked.

Following EasyStep Interview will result in a completed, correct tax return. Of course, as you gain experience, you can elect to bypass EasyStep Interview and use Forms Method where you have more direct control over the preparation of your return. Your chances for making mistakes increase in Forms Method.

TurboTax users have several ways to obtain answers to their tax questions. Along the right-hand side of all interview screens is a list of frequently-asked questions. Clicking on a question provides an instant answer. In addition, TurboTax has online help to aid you in using the software and a variety of worksheets designed to reduce complex tax laws to easy-to-follow steps. Chapters 3 and 4 provide examples and further explanation of TurboTax help and other aids.

The purpose of this chapter is to describe how to install TurboTax and provide an overview on using the software. If you are new to both TurboTax and tax return preparation, EasyStep Interview method is strongly recommended. As you become more familiar with tax return preparation and with the software, you can elect to use Forms Method. Forms Method takes less time, but requires a higher level of knowledge. In this manual, Chapter 3 is a detailed explanation of how to use EasyStep Interview. Chapter 4 covers Forms Method. Chapter 5 discusses how Intuit Inc. will help you use TurboTax and Chapter 6 includes problems to give you practice in using the software.

The topics discussed in this chapter are:

- Hardware Requirements for TurboTax
- How to install TurboTax using Windows 95 or 98
- Printing the Return
- Saving Taxpayer Data Files
- Quick Start to using EasyStep Interview

THE READ1040 FILE IS IMPORTANT

Information about the software that became available after the manual was printed is included in the READ1040 file on the CD-ROM. It is to your advantage to read this file prior to using TurboTax. After you install TurboTax, the READ1040 file is automatically stored in the TAX99 directory for your future reference.

HARDWARE REQUIREMENTS

TurboTax for Windows will operate with just about any hardware configuration that is compatible with Windows. The minimum hardware required for **this version** is listed below.

1. IBM PC or a compatible with a 486DX or higher processor Windows 95, Windows 98, Windows for Workgroup, or Windows NT 4.0
2. Minimum of 16 MB of RAM

3.   Minimum of 30 MB of available hard disk space
4.   2X CD-ROM drive with a minimum 300 KB-per-second sustained transfer rate (4X CD-ROM drive recommended)
5.   Electronic filing and online features require a 14400 baud (or faster) modem, or direct connection via a LAN (28800 baud is recommended)
6.   Windows-compatible printer
7.   An SVGA video card (minimum of 256 colors)

As indicated above, TurboTax will work with 16 megs of RAM. However, note that all Windows programs, including TurboTax, work **better** with more megs of RAM. Any new PC purchased in 2000 should have at least **64 megs** of RAM to efficiently run Windows software.

The end product of tax return preparation software is a fileable tax return, normally printed. For more information about printing, refer to the **File Print** command discussed in Chapter 4.

INSTALLATION OF TURBOTAX FOR WINDOWS 95/98

1.   Turn on your computer. Sit back and wait until the boot-up process is complete.

2.   Close all programs except Systray and Explorer. Disable all virus protection software.

3.   Insert the TurboTax CD-ROM into your drive. The installation process may begin automatically. If so, skip to Step 5, below. If not, proceed to Step 4, below.

4.   Click on the Start button located in the bottom left-hand corner of your screen. In the pop-up menu that appears, click on "Run ..." A "Run" dialog box will open, as shown below. If your CD-ROM drive is the f: drive, then in the input section in the middle of the dialog box, enter the following and then click OK   f:setup

If your CD-ROM drive is other than the f: drive, just use the appropriate letter in place of "f".

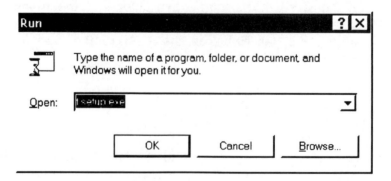

Figure 2-1 Run Dialog Box

5.   A "wizard" included on the CD-ROM will guide you through all installation steps. Just follow the instructions on the screen. Among the TurboTax icons created during this process is an Uninstall icon. You can click on this icon anytime in the future to uninstall TurboTax.

6.   To proceed from screen to screen, click on the Next button (or the Yes button). Read each screen. Several screens provide interesting information about TurboTax and other Intuit Inc. products. The installation process takes several minutes. Please be patient.

7.   The setup program creates the Program Group "TurboTax 1999" containing three (or more) program items and their related icons, similar to those shown below.

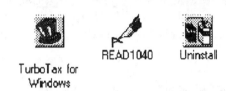

Figure 2-2 Program Group icons

The red, white and blue top hat is the icon for TurboTax for Windows. The READ1040 icon displays information about the latest changes in the program. The Uninstall icon allows you to remove TurboTax from your disk after you have completed this course and do not expect to be using it again in the near term.

8.   Once TurboTax is installed, it is ready to launch.

9.   At any time in the future, you can access TurboTax icons by first clicking on the Start button (located in the bottom left-hand corner of your screen). Then, click Program. Finally, click on TurboTax.

10.   If you receive a message that TurboTax did NOT install properly, refer to the section below, "What if My Software Won't Install?"

11.   Once installed, your computer is ready to launch TurboTax. Before using TurboTax, it is recommended that you read the first portion of Chapter 6 which provides a detailed example using EasyStep Interview.

What If My Software Won't Install?

You are likely reading this section because TurboTax did not install properly. First, rethink your steps. Did you miss one? For example, did you disable all virus-protection utilities and memory resident programs? Did you restart your PC after doing so?

Another problem can be space on your disk drive. If your hard disk is small by today's standards, this is a major problem for all Windows software. You need at least 30 megabytes of space on your hard drive to load TurboTax. There are various software alternatives for increasing hard drive capacity by compressing the hard drive.

The TurboTax Setup program installs TrueType fonts needed by TurboTax. If you receive an error message indicating that it could not install these fonts, you must install them manually by following the instructions in your Windows User Guide. Check the Printer Manager.

QUICK START TO USING TURBOTAX

You have the software installed. With any version of Windows, select the program group or folder titled, "TurboTax for Windows 1999." Click on the title or folder and then launch TurboTax by clicking on the red, white and blue hat icon. You will see a "Welcome to TurboTax" screen. Review your welcome. After you are done reading your welcome, click **Next**.

By default you start in **EasyStep Interview**. This approach, rather than using Forms Method, is the best way to start learning how to use TurboTax. While it may take you more time to complete your first return, TurboTax will walk you through the entire tax return preparation process. As explained earlier, EasyStep Interview asks you tax questions in plain English and, based upon your answers, decides which tax forms you need, does all the calculations, and fills in the forms for you. Your part is to read the screen before you press the enter key or click the mouse. If you read the entire screen, you will prevent most common errors. For more information, read Chapter 3, Using EasyStep Interview. If you decide to use Forms Method, read Chapter 4.

One of the last steps is for TurboTax to provide a "Final Review" of your return. The purpose of selecting this step is to allow TurboTax to check your return for errors. The program can not detect data entry errors, but it can check for errors of omission and illogical entries. Thus, if you check the "Single" filing status but you are married, TurboTax will not detect it. But, if you have checked Single and then attempt to enter a name for your spouse, TurboTax will give you an error message. Reviewing your return is highly recommended.

PRINTING THE RETURN

The final step is to print the tax return. Filing the return electronically is also an option. Before you print the tax return, however, you must inform TurboTax what printer you will be using. By default, TurboTax selects the printer you installed with Windows. That is, it uses the Windows Print Manager for printing. If you are still using the same printer, you do not need to set up the printer again. If it is necessary to change the selected printer, go to the Print Manager in Windows and change your printer. You can change the option at any time by simply repeating the process. If your specific printer is not on the list, select one that is compatible with it. Changing the printer will normally not be required. The problem can arise if you are in a lab with a variety of printers and there is no lab monitor to maintain proper printer installation.

You begin the printing process by selecting the **Print and File** option at the top of the screen. You are then given three options –

1.   File electronically
2.   Print my return to mail it
3.   Print my return for my records

Filing electronically is explained briefly in Chapter 1. Obviously, you would not choose this option for a typical homework problem. Option 2 prints only those tax forms and supporting schedules that are required to be filed. Option 3 prints everything Option 2 prints, plus it provides various supporting computations and schedules that are not required to be filed with the IRS but are helpful for understanding some of the tax return amounts.

SAVING FILES IN TURBOTAX

You can save as many files in the current directory as you desire. Also, you select the filename. TurboTax adds the filetype "TAX," but you can identify the return any way you desire. It is recommended that you use some part of the taxpayer's name. For example when you do Mary Brown's return in Chapter 6, you should use the name "MBROWN" as your file name. At the time you save the file, you will have to specify the desired directory if you want to save the file in another directory. For example, if you wanted to save MBROWN on a floppy disk in the A drive, you would specify the file name as **A:\MBROWN**. The actual filename will be "MBROWN.TAX" and you will be able to find it when you use the **File Open** option. The file contains only the data; the actual tax form itself is not saved with the data. When you open the file, its data is added to the appropriate forms throughout in the program.

TURBOTAX HELP

Help with TurboTax is available in different forms. First, Chapters 3 and 4 of this manual act as a reference. Each command is discussed, including both how to use the command and when it should be used. Second, TurboTax has an extensive online Help function that is designed to give you online assistance while you operate the program. Help is selected from the main menu or from the Help button displayed with the forms. Also, several features of TurboTax are designed to help you complete the return. These help features are discussed below.

EasyStep Interview -- This option is an interactive question and answer format that is designed to help you identify and complete the correct forms. (Note, it can be selected when you first enter TurboTax, or later after you have completed part of the return using Forms Method.) If you want to take a break and return to the forms later, TurboTax will remember where you left off and put you in that same location the next time you load TurboTax.

Frequently asked questions – These are located in the upper right-hand portion of EasyStep Interview screens. Clicking once on these questions provides answers instantly.

Final Review – This option finds various logical errors and inconsistencies in the information you have provided. Missing information is also identified.

Tax help -- This options tells you how to enter information in the currently displayed form, and explains what TurboTax does with the information you enter. It is context sensitive, thus TurboTax interprets the current field on the tax form and provides the help needed.

Data Source -- This selection lists the **source** of the information that TurboTax transfers to the current line of the tax form which is marked with the cursor.

Government (IRS) Instructions -- This selection causes TurboTax to display the IRS instructions for the form shown on the screen. With the state version of TurboTax, the government instructions are those of that state. For a New York return, the IRS instructions would be of limited use.

Program Help -- Should you need help understanding how TurboTax itself works, select this help tab.

In Chapter 5, the help available directly from the Intuit Inc. Customer Service support group is discussed. There, the telephone numbers for the various kinds of help are listed. Intuit Inc. is committed to supporting you even though your software was purchased from South-Western College Publishing.

TURBOTAX ON THE WORLD WIDE WEB

For more information about Intuit Inc. products, including TurboTax, see their sites on the World Wide Web at the following URLs:

> http://www.turbotax.com
> http://www.intuit.com

The TurboTax web site is available 24-hours a day, seven days a week. In this time of changing tax laws, it is good to have a source that is committed to keeping you up-to-date on law changes.

CONCLUDING COMMENTS

The purpose of this chapter is to help you install TurboTax for Windows and to give you a brief overview of how it works. If you are experienced using Windows software and using a mouse, you should be able to load the software and follow the on-screen instructions. As with any new software, you need to have the mind set of try and try again. Computers do not get upset if you make an error, so why should you? Simply press the ESC key or click on **Cancel**, and try it again.

If you are an experienced Windows user, you are ready to get started. If you follow your instincts and expect the keys to work in TurboTax like the keys function in other Windows software, you will not be disappointed. The following chapters cover the commands and their use: Chapter 3 is for EasyStep Interview, and Chapter 4 for Forms Method. Good Luck!

CHAPTER 3

USING EASYSTEP® INTERVIEW

Once you have TurboTax installed you are ready to complete a return. TurboTax provides two approaches to completing a tax return - **EasyStep Interview** and **Forms Method.** EasyStep Interview is described in this chapter. Use of Forms Method is discussed in Chapter 4. As the name implies, EasyStep Interview is easier to use than Forms Method, although it can take more time to complete a tax return. Because of its ease of use, it is recommended that you start with EasyStep Interview.

EasyStep Interview turns the tax return preparation process into a series of simple steps. TurboTax walks you through the tax return in a question/answer format. TurboTax provides the questions in simple English and you provide the answers. Then TurboTax takes your answers and places them on the appropriate line on the correct form. Numbers are added or subtracted as necessary; totals are transferred from detailed worksheets to specific forms and from specific forms to summary forms. Along the way, TurboTax makes suggestions regarding your answers. In some cases, TurboTax will make a selection for you based upon generally accepted tax planning. Of course, you can change any selection made by TurboTax. When you have finished your interview, TurboTax checks for missing information, and then tells you how to print the return. Keep in mind that if you answer questions incorrectly, errors will occur. Thus, it is very important to read the entire question carefully before you press enter or click on the mouse.

TO BEGIN -- LOAD THE SOFTWARE

In Windows 95/98, execute the following steps:

1. Click on the "Start" icon.

2. Move the mouse pointer to the "Programs," then to the "TurboTax for Windows 1999" folder title and then to "1999 TurboTax for Windows" with the red, white and blue TurboTax for Windows icon. Once the pointer is pointing to TurboTax, click your mouse.

3. TurboTax is loaded. You are immediately welcomed and invited to click on the "Let's Get Started" button. On the next screen, click on the "Start My Return" button.

You have the option to view various screens containing background information. You have the opportunity to load tax information from your last year's tax return. For classroom tax return problems, there is normally not a prior year's return available. Thus, click on the "Skip transfer" and "Skip import" buttons when then appear. Continue to click on the appropriate buttons to proceed to the "Your Filing Status" screen. This is where you begin to input information to TurboTax. To remain with EasyStep Interview, provide the information requested on each screen and then press the "Continue" button to proceed.

The next chapter discusses how to leave EasyStep Interview to use Forms Method. Briefly, this is done by either clicking on the gray "Go to Forms ..." button in the Forms window on the bottom of the screen, or clicking on the Forms menu option in the top left-hand corner of the screen (and then clicking on "Go To Forms" in the drop-down menu).

BASICS OF EASYSTEP INTERVIEW

Money magazine periodically reviews the leading personal tax return preparation software packages. According to *Money* (January 1994), ". . . all of the top programs use the approach pioneered by TurboTax: an automated interview in which your PC asks you a long list of tax-related questions and fills in the appropriate lines on the forms." Interview is the focus of EasyStep Interview and when you use it, you will see why others praise it.

Figure 3-1 (on the next page) is an example of a typical screen in EasyStep Interview. At the very top, we see that "TurboTax for Windows" is the program currently running. Once tax return data are saved, the filename of the data is displayed. The second row of the screen lists the first TurboTax menu. While using EasyStep Interview, you will rarely need this menu. The next row shows the tabs for the nine steps of EasyStep Interview. These steps are: Personal Info, Income, Deductions, Taxes/Credits, Misc., Final Review, State Taxes, Print and File, Finish. Detailed information about these steps is provided later.

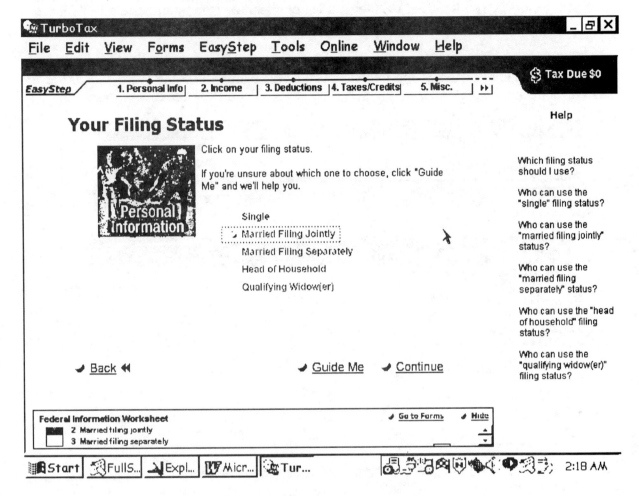

Figure 3-1 Typical EasyStep Interview screen

The large bold blue type identifies your current interview topic, which is "Your Filing Status" in Figure 3-1. Tax return sections are shown in the EasyStep Progress Bar, the fourth line down from the top of the screen, numbered one through five. "Your Filing Status" is part of tax return section 1 Personal Info. The other tax return sections are 2 Income; 3 Deductions; 4 Taxes/Credits; and 5 Misc. Following the 5 Misc button is a double-arrowed button. Clicking on it reveals the remaining tax return section buttons - 6 Final Review; 7 State Taxes; 8 Print and File; and 9 Finish. When you can see buttons 5-9, the double-arrowed button is located to the left of the 5 Misc button. Clicking on it will reveal buttons 1-5 again.

Clicking on any of the tax return section buttons opens the EasyStep Navigator window which enables you to navigate or jump to any part of the tax return preparation process. All tax return steps are listed in the EasyStep Navigator. The scroll bar on the right-hand side of the window allows you to access any step. If you have a particular topic in mind and you do not see it listed, you can type the topic in the small Search window at the top of the EasyStep Navigator window. You will then be shown a list of interview steps that pertain to your topic. You can then click on the step to which you want to proceed.

For example, assume you bought a home this year and you paid points on your mortgage. If you want to jump to part of the interview regarding points, type the word "points" in the Search window, then click on the Search button. You will then see the following screen:

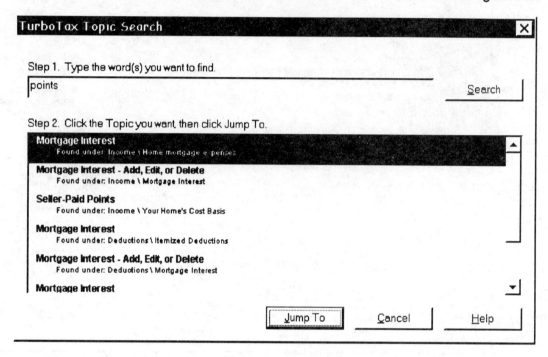

Figure 3-2 TurboTax Topic Search screen

In the second box in the Search screen window you will find all of the locations in the interview that pertain to points. Click on the interview location of interest. Then, click on the "Jump To" button under the Step 2 box.

The gray "Help" button on the right-hand side of EasyStep Interview (Figure 3-1) enables you to access an extensive electronic library of tax information. The information you see immediately after clicking on "Help" pertains to the current interview screen. But once the Help window opens, you can access help on virtually any tax topic. The Help window on the next page is associated with the interview screen in Figure 3-1.

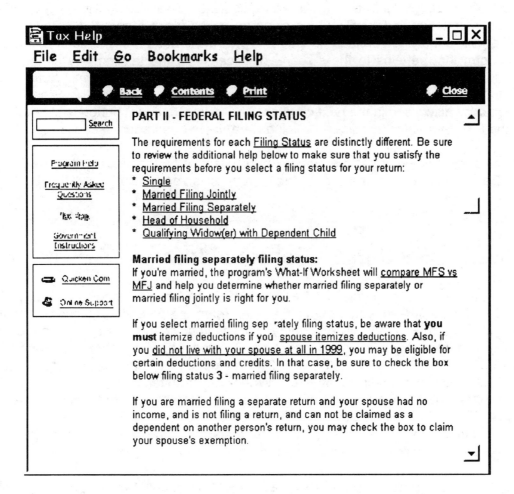

Figure 3-3 Help window

Since the EasyStep Interview screen in Figure 3-1 pertains to filing status, the help window provides information regarding the five filing status categories. You can read the information on the screen and use the scroll bar in the right-hand side of the screen to see additional related information. The blue underlined words are "hot links" to further explanations.

The "Contents" button and "Search" window in the Tax Help window enable you to access other areas of the help "library." In addition, by clicking on the "Government Instructions" button on the left-hand side of the window, you can access the actual government tax form instructions pertaining to the topic when such instructions are available. If you need help using TurboTax, click on the "Program Help" button. As you can see from the top portion of the window, TurboTax help supports bookmarking and printing. All of these features provide a powerful and user-friendly library of valuable tax information. Another way to find answers to tax questions is by clicking on the "Frequently Asked Questions" button.

The middle of the EasyStep Interview screen in Figure 3-1 is a "Dialog Area." This is where you provide information to TurboTax by clicking on boxes (as in Figure 3-1), providing dollar amounts, and/or supplying verbal information. Toward the bottom of the screen is a portion of the tax form that pertains to the screen. You can hide the tax form by clicking on the "Hide" button or you can view the entire form by clicking on the "Go to Forms" button. Going to forms enables you to work directly with tax forms rather than using EasyStep Interview. Forms Method is discussed in the next chapter. The blue "Continue" button is clicked after all items in the EasyStep Interview screen "Dialog Area" have been addressed.

The discussion below pertains to the nine tax return section buttons included in the EasyStep Program Bar located across the top of the TurboTax screen. Buttons 1-5 are shown in Figure 3-1.

Tax Return Section 1 - Personal Info

The first tax return section button is 1 Personal Info. This section begins with a Welcome screen. On the next screen, you can begin the tax return preparation process by clicking on the "Start My Return" button. After another introductory screen, you have the option of transferring data from your prior year's tax return. To start a new tax return, click on the "Skip Transfer" button. Note, however, that the transfer option in TurboTax is one of the real powers of using tax preparation software. When you transfer last year's data, you save significant data entry. Data such as your name, address, sources of income, listed deductions, depreciation schedules, and so on are added to your current year return. The data that changes between years, such as dollar amounts of income, will not be transferred, but all of the text data will automatically be entered for the current year.

One additional note. Because TurboTax is designed for individual taxpayers who typically file only one return, it expects that you will complete only your own personal tax return. Thus, after you complete or simply work on a return, that last return worked on will automatically be loaded when you start TurboTax. For the second and later returns, you will have to click on the "Start My Return" button.

You are then given the opportunity to import tax return data from other Intuit products, such as Quicken and QuickBooks. Click on the "Skip Import" button to proceed to the next screen. On the next screen, click on the "Continue My Return" button.

The next screen, "Your Filing Status," begins the actual tax return preparation process. As you move through the initial screens of the interview, you can see the form or worksheet being completed at the bottom of the screen if you click on the "show tax form" button.

Tax Return Sections 2-5

Once all Personal Information is entered, the Interview proceeds through tax return sections 2-5, listed below:

   2. Income
   3. Deductions
   4. Taxes/Credits
   5. Misc.

As you proceed through the Interview screens you will see two basic types of screens. The first type is in a multiple choice format. Here TurboTax asks objective, closed-end questions. You respond by pointing to your answer with the mouse and clicking. TurboTax will normally suggest an answer, the default answer, indicated by a dotted-line box around the answer. If the default answer is acceptable, you may press the enter key to select it and move on. You can select any answer by pointing to the answer and clicking the mouse once.

The second type of screen asks you to input data in data entry boxes. TurboTax will move you through each in the order of left to right and top to bottom. As you enter data, it is placed on the appropriate line on the form displayed in the lower half of the screen.

Tax Return Section 6 - Final Review

Tax return section buttons 6-9 are accessed by clicking on the double-arrowed button to the right of the 5 Misc button. The purpose of the Final Review section is for TurboTax to check the return for errors. TurboTax conducts the following types of reviews:

   1.   Error Check -- contradictory or missing entries.
   2.   Deduction Finder -- deductions you may have overlooked.
   3.   Audit Alerts and Overrides -- situations that might provoke an IRS audit or inquiry. These suggestions are based upon norms for given income levels.
   4.   U.S. Averages — Your tax return items will be compared in columnar format with the average items for a taxpayer with similar adjusted gross income. The purpose of the comparison is just for your information. While it is true that the IRS audit selection programs use this type of information to select returns for audit, your goal is to prepare a return that is correct. Thus, the probability of an audit is not relevant to you. At least, it should not be relevant.
   5.   Tax Report -- a printable plan of action and tips to help save on next year's taxes.

The results of Audit Flags, Tax Savings Ideas, and Deductions Finder reviews are for information only; no changes are required. When you reach the Final Review step, you will have the option of selecting any or all of the above four types of reviews. You simply click on the box next to the type of review. For the first few returns, I suggest that you select all Reviews so that you will be familiar with the type of information available.

Generally, you will discover that you failed to check a required box or to provide some other required information. In EasyStep Interview you will be led to the interview step where the error is addressed and given an opportunity to correct the error. The instructions will be displayed on the screen, so all you have to do is click on the Next button and read the screen. The items identified by the Final Review are listed one problem at a time, in a dialog box. When you are using Forms Method, you can click on the Forms Menu Option, Form Errors. TurboTax moves you to the appropriate line on the appropriate form where you can edit the line to fix the problem.

Tax Return Section 7 - State Taxes

Typically, for class purposes you do not complete the associated state return. With TurboTax, the state return is a companion program and is not available from South-Western College Publishing. If you want to purchase the state module, all the information you need can be found on the Web at www.quickenstore.com. The state module works in the same way as the federal module. Data from the federal return is automatically transferred to the state return. The degree of integration is wonderful. Intuit Inc. has done a good job of facilitating the preparation of state tax returns.

Tax Return Section 8 - Print and File

The final step is to print the tax return. Filing the return electronically is also an option. Before you print the tax return, however, you must inform TurboTax what printer you will be using. By default, TurboTax selects the printer you installed with Windows. That is, it uses the Windows Print Manager to do printing. If you are still using the same printer, you do not need to set up the printer again. If it is necessary to change the selected printer, go to the Print Manager in Windows and change your printer. You can change the option at any time by simply repeating the process. If your specific printer is not on the list, select one that is compatible with it. Changing the printer will normally not be required. The problem can arise if you are in a lab with a variety of printers and no lab monitor to maintain proper printer installation.

You begin the printing process by selecting the Print and File button at the top of the screen. You are then given three options –

1. Electronic Filing
2. Print for Mailing
3. Print for Your Records

Filing electronically is explained briefly in Chapter 1. Obviously, you would not choose this option for a typical homework problem. Option 2 prints only those tax forms and supporting schedules that are required to be filed. Options 3 prints everything Option 2 prints, plus it provides various supporting computations and schedules that are not required to be filed with the IRS but are helpful for understanding some of the tax return amounts.

If you select Option 2, you are then given the option to print using "1040PC format" rather than the standard tax return format. Form 1040PC returns are condensed to three columns per page. This format takes far less paper than the conventional format. See Figure 3-4 PC Format, below. A Form 1040PC-format return is only created after you complete the return. It really is just a print option and not an alternative to the Form 1040. Most returns can be printed in one or two pages if the 1040PC format is selected. Check with your professor to see if he or she wishes you to submit returns formatted as 1040PCs. If so you will save a great deal of printing time and paper.

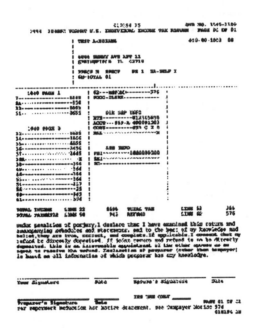

Figure 3-4 PC Format

Increasingly the IRS is making it possible to file your return electronically. By the year 2003, electronic filing is predicted to be the preferred choice of most taxpayers. TurboTax enables electronic filing of both Federal and State returns. The fee for processing Federal returns is $9.95. For State returns, the fee is $4.95. TurboTax transmits the return via the web to the Intuit Electronic Filing Center using a secure Internet connection. The return is then converted to a standardized format and transferred to the IRS or State taxing authority. Most taxpayers must follow up electronic filing with a one-page paper tax form (Form 8453-OL and, in some cases, attachments). The main reason for the paper form is to provide a signature to the IRS. In contrast, some taxpayers are selected by the IRS to completely avoid paper filings. Such taxpayers receive an official letter from the IRS giving them an *e-file* Customer Number (called an ECN). TurboTax prompts taxpayers to enter their ECN if they have one.

Currently the IRS insists upon a "middle man" for electronic processing because it lacks the hardware to handle the number of filers if each taxpayer could file directly to the IRS electronically. The GAO has been critical of this policy. Of course, for academic purposes, filing will consist of submitting a return to your instructor and normally it will be on paper. Thus, you will not use this option. Again, the PC format will save paper.

Tax Return Section 9 - Finish

Once you have completed this year's return, it is time to start looking to next year. The Finish option tells you that you can use the TurboTax W-4 Worksheet and Estimated Tax Worksheet in connection with the remaining months of the <u>current</u> tax year. You may click on "Help" for more information about these features.

CONCLUDING COMMENTS

EasyStep Interview is designed to be used by the typical taxpayer. Certainly, you have more tax training than the typical taxpayer. Try to have patience as you learn to use this powerful technology. Keep in mind that TurboTax is the very best tax return preparation software in the country for individual tax returns. Thus, your investment of time into learning how to use the TurboTax program is worthwhile. As you prepare tax returns, recall that you have a tax textbook to search for the correct tax treatment of many transactions. Consult your textbook as well as the various help facilities in TurboTax if you have questions.

Good Luck!

CHAPTER 4

USING FORMS METHOD

EasyStep Interview discussed in Chapter 3 provides you with an interview that takes your answers to questions and enters the information on the appropriate tax form. As you become more familiar with the forms and the required information, you will likely find that Forms Method discussed in this chapter will ordinary take less time than EasyStep Interview. This is because it is generally faster to directly access the correct form and enter the necessary information than answer EasyStep Interview questions about the form.

TO BEGIN -- LOAD THE SOFTWARE

In Windows 95/98, execute the following steps:

1.   Click on the "Start" icon.

2.   Move the mouse pointer to the "Programs," then to the "TurboTax for Windows 1999" folder title and then to "1999 TurboTax for Windows" with the red, white and blue TurboTax for Windows icon. Once the pointer is pointing to TurboTax, click your mouse.

3.   TurboTax is loaded. You are immediately welcomed and invited to click on the "Let's Get Started" button. On the next screen, click on the "Start My Return" button.

4.   To begin Forms Method, click on the Forms menu item at the top of the screen. In the drop-down menu that appears, click on the first option, "Go To Forms."

5.   The first form you see is the "Federal Information Worksheet."

WHERE TO BEGIN

As indicated above, the first form is the Federal Information Worksheet. All identifying information is entered on this worksheet. For example, this is the worksheet where you enter your name and address and indicate your filing status and exemptions.

When you come to the bottom of the worksheet, you will see a box titled "QuickZoom to Form 1040." The QuickZoom® feature is used throughout TurboTax to move from summary schedules and forms to the supporting worksheets and schedules. If there is a supporting form or worksheet for any line on a form, the phrase "Click the attached button to view the supporting field" will appear on the status line, the last row of the screen.

The QuickZoom feature is fundamental to Forms Method. Form 1040 is the general summary form for all tax returns. Once you move to Form 1040, the procedure to follow is to go down Form 1040 line by line. When you come to an income item that applies to you, double click on the small magnifying glass icon, adjacent to the current field, to quick zoom to the supporting forms or worksheets. When you complete the supporting form, close it by clicking on the "Close Form" button at the top of the form. You will then move to the higher level form, returning to Form 1040 when all support forms are closed. Then move to the next applicable line. You continue through Form 1040 until you have completed your tax return.

As you complete the forms and schedules, you will note that TurboTax has added detail boxes, called "smart worksheets," to the forms and schedules for your convenience. The purpose is to give you more guidance and room to include your transactions. These added boxes will not print when you print your return. They are there only for your convenience.

Two important aids need to be emphasized. One is the Open Form Menu, accessed by clicking on the "Forms" menu item at the top of the screen. The purpose of Open Form Menu is to give you a list of all forms available for completion with this version of TurboTax. If you know which form you need to complete, Schedule C for business income for example, you can move directly to the form by using this menu. Clicking on the Forms menu item also provides an option to view the entire tax return ("Show My Return ...").

There will likely be occasions when you do not know or do not recall the appropriate form to use for a tax return item. The Tools menu option, Topic Search, is designed to help you identify the form you need. The option works like most search options in Windows based software. Selecting the Topic Search option opens a dialog box with two response boxes. In the first, you enter a key word or phrase (such as "points"). TurboTax will search the listing of topics and display those that match your request in the second response box. You select the one you want and click on the "Jump To" button at the bottom of the dialog box. TurboTax then provides further guidance for the item. If your search does not produce the desired results, try using different key words or phrases.

At any time you can move to EasyStep Interview to complete any part of a return by clicking on the gray "Back to Interview" button in the upper right-hand corner of the screen. If you want to use EasyStep Interview for only one form, you can complete that form with the help of the interview and then click on the "Go to Forms" button to return to Forms Method.

DATA ENTRY USING FORMS METHOD

The TurboTax screen typically displays only part of a tax form, schedule or worksheet. The display acts as a window through which the form is viewed, similar to viewing different parts of an electronic spreadsheet. The user can move up or down the form with the normal movement keys -- the scroll bar at the right of the screen, Up Arrow, Down Arrow, Page Up or Page Down keys.

The specific areas on the tax forms, schedules and worksheets that are designed to receive information are referred to as fields. TurboTax uses a box with white background as a field indicator to highlight the current location of the cursor. The width of the cursor corresponds to the width of the field to which data will be entered. If you enter text data, TurboTax will vary the point size so that the data will fit the space available.

The forms on the screen have six types of fields:

- Text Input Fields
- Numeric Input Fields
- Calculated Value Fields
- Itemized Value Fields
- Overridden Value Fields
- QuickZoom Fields

Each of these fields are discussed below. The type of field will be indicated on the status bar, the last row on the screen, at the left-hand corner of that row.

Text Input Fields

Text input fields are the areas into which you enter text information such as names, dates, addresses and descriptions. The current field is highlighted by the box field cursor. If the field is a transferred field, it is "non-enterable." Thus, you will not be able to enter any data in that field. You will see that such fields have a dark-line box around the field and on the left side of the status bar at the bottom of the screen, you will see the sentence "TurboTax automatically calculates this value for you." If you attempt to enter data, TurboTax displays a note suggesting that you click on the attach button to view the supporting data. To overwrite the field, you click on the right button and select the "Override" option. It is not a good idea to override fields. If the field is an enterable field, you can re-enter data by simply typing in the highlighted field.

Numeric Input Fields

Numeric input fields are the areas into which you enter numbers. If nothing has been entered, the field is blank. If the field is enterable, it will have a field indicator box around it. In the lower left hand corner, the status bar will advise you to "Type in a number." Negative numbers are entered by pressing the minus sign and then the number. Commas are appropriately added by TurboTax when you press the Enter key. To enter cents, you must enter the decimal. Percentages must be entered in their decimal form, thus ".1" is entered for 10 percent. The numbers can be changed by simply entering the correct amount in the same field, thereby replacing the earlier data. TurboTax will "round off" cents to dollars when transferring some data between forms.

Calculated Value Fields

Calculated value fields can be either text or numeric values that are automatically calculated by TurboTax based upon data you have entered. The values are carried forward from other forms or computed from the information on the current form. You can not make entry to these fields except by using the Override feature. Normally you do not wish to do that. The field indicator box for calculated value fields is a thick dark box around the field.

Itemized Value Fields

TurboTax provides the capability to prepare an itemized list of items and total the amounts. The totals are then entered in the numeric field supported by the itemized list. To create an itemized listing simply click on the small itemized statement icon that is adjacent to the field. Clicking the icon will open an itemized statement for your use.

Overridden Value Fields

At times you may make an error in a supporting schedule and want to just correct the total and not bother with correcting the supporting schedule. This is not good. To do so creates bad habits and is an incorrect use of the flexibility in TurboTax. However, there are some occasions where TurboTax does not provide for a rarely used allocation method and you will have to override a calculated value in order to get your desired results. The Override option under the Edit Menu allows you this flexibility. (You can also select Override by clicking on the right button of the mouse and then select the Override option.) If you override a field, a note on the status bar (at the bottom of the screen) saying, "You have replaced the value automatically calculated by TurboTax" will appear. With a color monitor, Overridden fields are displayed in Red. It is rarely necessary to use the Override feature; do so with caution.

Formatting Data

TurboTax will automatically format data to its common forms. Thus, Social Security or Federal Employer's ID numbers are formatted automatically. Also, for numeric entries over 1,000, TurboTax will insert the appropriate commas. Negative numbers are simply entered with a leading minus sign.

Date fields are used in some forms. Dates must be entered in the form "mm/dd/yy," so that TurboTax can properly compute depreciation deductions and other related calculations. If the month or day is only one digit, you must add a leading zero. Thus, January 1, 1999, must be entered as 01/01/99.

Checking Boxes

Frequently you will be required to check boxes to indicate your selection. For example, the filing status is indicated by checking the box by the status name. To check the box, simply move the pointer to the box and click once. Clicking a second time will remove the check. If multiple boxes can be checked, simply move to the next one and click. If only one box can be checked, your first check will be removed when you enter the second check. Similarly, if you are required to enter a Yes or No, you can click in the box labeled "Yes."

THE COLOR OF FIELDS

TurboTax displays certain types of fields in different colors as your cursor highlights them. With practice you will be able to recognize the source of the entry by these colors. The two major colors are blue, which indicates data that you have entered, and black, the color used for calculated values.

Color	Type of Entry
Blue	Data entered by you
Black	Data calculated or transferred by TurboTax
Green	Data imported from another program
Purple	Amount from an itemization (supporting details list)
Aqua	Data transferred from last year's file, or from a federal return to a state return
Red	Calculated value overridden by you, or an error
Red *Italicized*	An entry marked as estimated by you

USE OF THE KEYBOARD

The mouse is the primary means of operating TurboTax. However, much of the data you enter is done with the keyboard. You will find that the keys are used in a manner similar to many business software products. Below is a listing of the keys and their use in TurboTax.

<ENTER> -- Used to indicate that you have completed entering a field, or that you have selected a command. By default, TurboTax automatically moves the cursor to the next field after you press the enter key. The order of movement is from top to bottom and from left to right.

<TAB> -- As with other Windows software, the TAB key is used to move between options within dialog boxes.

Each of the menu options have speed keys, a combination of the Control key and a letter. These keys can be used in the place of selecting from the menu or icons. For example, Ctrl A will access the Open Form menu. If you use TurboTax for a period of time, you will find these keys very useful.

WORKSHEETS AND FORMS

Inputting tax data follows the flow of paper tax returns. To make it easier to enter certain types of information, TurboTax uses a variety of worksheets. The worksheets are listed in the Open Form menu under the form or schedule they support. The entries you make on the worksheets result in entries on the tax forms. You will greatly appreciate these worksheets when you work with the more complicated areas of income taxes, such as passive activities.

A second type of worksheet, referred to as a "Smart Worksheet," appears on some of the forms themselves. These smart worksheets are short and relate to the form currently in use. They will not be printed on the face of the form; they are printed separately. You can hide or show the display of smart worksheets at any time by selecting the appropriate setting in the View menu, click Smart Worksheets. However, they are provided to help you. TurboTax strongly encourages you to leave the display of the smart worksheets on, and there is no advantage to not using them.

TurboTax supports up to ten W-2 forms. To enter the second or more, simply double click on Line 7 of Form 1040. The screen will display a dialog box that lists all W-2's that have been entered. You will be requested to select one of the listed W-2's or to create a new W-2. The same procedure is used for Forms 1099, that report interest income; and K-1's that report income from partnerships, S Corporations, and estates and trusts. The worksheets created appear on the screen in the same format as the paper source document, thus data entry is made easy -- you just fill in the blanks. The individual forms are summarized by TurboTax on summary worksheets and then the totals are transferred to Form 1040 or other appropriate schedule. The system supports all lines on a K-1 form, thus rather complex transactions are made simple -- TurboTax takes the information from the K-1 and puts it on the appropriate form even if it involves passive losses or alternative minimum tax.

PRINTING THE RETURN

The final step is to print the tax return. Filing the return electronically is also an option. Before you print the tax return, however, you must inform TurboTax what printer you will be using. By default, TurboTax selects the printer you installed with Windows. That is, it uses the Windows Print Manager to do printing. If you are still using the same printer, you do not need to set up the printer again. If it is necessary to change the selected printer, go to the Print Manager in Windows and change your printer. You can change the option at any time by simply repeating the process. If your specific printer is not on the list, select one that is compatible with it. Changing the printer will normally not be required. The problem can arise if you are in a lab with a variety of printers and no lab monitor to maintain proper printer installation.

You begin the printing process by selecting the Print and File option at the top of the screen. You are then given three options –

      1.   Electronic Filing
      2.   Print for Mailing
      3.   Print for Your Records

Filing electronically is explained briefly in Chapter 1. Obviously, you would not choose this option for a typical homework problem. Option 2 prints only those tax forms and supporting schedules that are required to be filed. Options 3 prints everything Option 2 prints, plus it provides various supporting computations and schedules that are not required to be filed with the IRS but are helpful for understanding some of the tax return amounts.

If you select Option 2, you are then given the option to print using "1040PC format" rather than the standard tax return format. Form 1040PC returns are condensed to three columns per page. This format takes far less paper than the conventional format. See Figure 4-1 PC Format, below. You can still select it from the File Print menu option or the File & Print tab. A Form 1040PC-format return is only created after you complete the return. It really is just a print option and not an alternative to the Form 1040. Most returns can be printed in one or two pages if the 1040PC format is selected. Check with your professor to see if he or she wishes you to submit returns formatted as 1040PCs. If so you will save a great deal of printing time and paper.

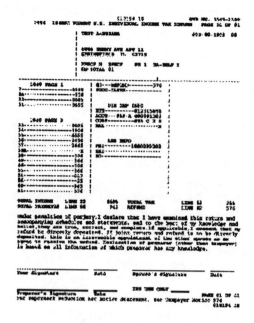

Figure 4-1 PC Format

Increasingly the IRS is making it possible to file your return electronically. By the year 2003, electronic filing is predicted to be the preferred choice of most taxpayers. TurboTax enables electronic filing of both Federal and State returns. The fee for processing Federal returns is $9.95. For State returns, the fee is $4.95. TurboTax transmits the return via the web to the Intuit Electronic Filing Center using a secure Internet connection.   The return is then converted to a standardized format and transferred to the IRS or State taxing authority. Most taxpayers must follow up electronic filing with a one-page paper tax form (Form 8453-OL and, in some cases, attachments).   The main reason for the paper form is to provide a signature to the IRS.   In contrast, some taxpayers are selected by the IRS to completely avoid paper filings. Such taxpayers receive an official letter from the IRS giving them an *e-file* Customer Number (called an ECN).   TurboTax prompts taxpayers to enter their ECN if they have one.

Currently the IRS insists upon a "middle man" for electronic processing because it lacks the hardware to handle the number of filers if each taxpayer could file directly to the IRS electronically. The GAO has been critical of this policy. Of course, for academic purposes, filing will consist of submitting a return to your instructor and normally it will be on paper. Thus, you will not use this option. Again, the PC format will save paper.

SAVING FILES IN TURBOTAX

You can save as many files in the current directory as you desire. Also, you select the filename. TurboTax adds the filetype "TAX," but you can identify the return any way you desire. It is recommended that you use some part of the taxpayer's name. For example when you prepare Mary Brown's return in Chapter 6, you should use the name "MBROWN" as your file name. At the time you save the file, you will have to specify the desired directory if you want to save the file in another directory. For example, if you wanted to save MBROWN on a floppy disk in the A drive, you would specify the file name as A:\MBROWN. The actual filename will be "MBROWN.TAX" and you will be able to find it when you use the File Open option. The file contains only the data; the actual tax form itself is not saved with the data. When you open the file, data is added to the appropriate forms throughout in the program.

TURBOTAX COMMANDS

Forms Method expects you to interact with the TurboTax commands. Most of the commands are self-explanatory. In fact many of the commands are common to all Windows software. The purpose of this section is to discuss each of the commands available in TurboTax. The commands are discussed in some length; perhaps more than you need. A more concise description of the commands is in Figure 4-2. The discussion that follows is intended to be a reference section, one that you will refer to often, but not necessarily read at one sitting.

The commands help you to use Forms Method. The focus of Forms Method is to fill out the appropriate tax forms. As such, you have to decide what form to use for a given transaction and then follow the instructions on the form to correctly report that transaction. TurboTax helps you in several ways. If there are several steps to completing the form, TurboTax provides a separate worksheet that breaks the form into various parts so that you can enter the data in the simplest way possible. The worksheet summarizes information and records it on the appropriate line on the form. You also have the Tools command option, Topic Search, that helps you find the correct place to report a transaction. When you find your topic, TurboTax moves you from Forms Method to EasyStep Interview where you are led through the transaction. If you do not want to be led, you can click on the "Go to Forms" button in the lower left hand corner and return to the form.

Figure 4-2 TurboTax Commands

Menu	Command	Function
File	New Tax Return	To begin a new tax return
	Open Tax Return	To open an existing tax return, one that has been previously worked on
	Save	Saves a tax return data file to disk using same name as current file
	Save As	Saves tax return with a different name
	Go to Fed	Toggles between state and federal tax return (available only in Forms Method)
	Go to State/City	Toggles between state and federal tax return (available only in Forms Method)
	Remove State/City	Erases data for state return
	Transfer '98	Transfers carryover tax data from prior year TurboTax tax data file
	TaxLink Import	Creates links between accounting software such as Quicken or QuickBooks and TurboTax
	TXF Import	Copies data from accounting software to TurboTax
	Remove All Imported Data	Deletes data from tax return data that has been imported
	Print	Opens the File Print dialog box which allows you to print tax return or selected forms
	Print Setup	Modifies settings for printer
	Print Test Page	Prints a test page to confirm your printer is correctly installed
	Electronic Filing	Interfaces with TurboTax electronic filing service
	Exit	Closes TurboTax. Gives opportunity to save a file before closing.
Edit	Undo	Removes last entry
	Cut, Copy, Paste	Common Windows commands to use clipboard for moving data around
	Override	Allows user to write over fields whose data are transferred from elsewhere

Edit	Add Supporting Detail	Used to add an itemization list to support data entered in a field
	Mark Estimated	Marks a field as estimated data. Estimates will appear as errors in Review
	Sort Table	Sorts a listing of data items
	Delete Table Row	Erases one row of a table
View	Smart Worksheets	Links to smart worksheets
	Tool Bar	Enables user to open and close tool bar
	Error Alerts	Provides notice of errors to user
	Status Bar	Provides status of return
	Hide Tax Form	Hides tax form
Forms	Go to Forms	Toggles between Forms Method and EasyStep Interview
	Open a Form	Opens listing of all available forms from which user may select a specific form
	Show My Return	Opens a listing of forms that are used with the current tax return
	QuickZoom	Moves from higher level form to supporting form or worksheet
	Remove (name of form or worksheet)	Allows user to delete current form
	Link Field	Allows user to link the current field to data from an accounting software such as QuickBooks.
	Select Line	Moves to a specified field on the current form
	Forms Errors	Displays a list of errors in tax return
	Find Next Error	Moves to next field in current form that has an error in the data for that field
	New Copy, Next Copy, Previous Copy	Moves between multiple worksheets such as W-2 worksheets, K-1 worksheets, etc
	Magnify all forms	Increases or decreases size of data in field

EasyStep	Back to interview	Continues EasyStep Interview where you left off when file was saved
	Guide Me	Opens detailed interview for current form, used with Forms Method
	1 - 9 steps	The steps in EasyStep Interview
Tools	My Tax Data	Lists data for current tax return, how it was entered, and where it appears in return
	Final Review	Performs a software check of return
	Topics Search	Opens list of topics and moves you to the correct location in EasyStep Interview for the data
	Calculator	Opens an on-screen calculator - *nice*
	Tax Summary	Displays current value of key lines of the current tax return
	What-if Worksheet	Used for tax planning. Displays for alternatives for selected tax lines
	History Report	Displays data for a total of five years of returns
Online	Internet, TurboTax Web Site, and other internet options	Provides a variety of internet options.
Window	Tile, Cascade, Arrange Icons, Close Window, Close All Windows	Same Windows options as are available with all Windows software. Impacts how your screen will appear
Help	Frequently Asked Questions	Opens a window of Frequently Asked Questions and answers
	Tax Help	TurboTax's tax related topics presented with a search window
	Government instructions	IRS instructions relating to current form
	Data Source	Displays where the data came from
	Program Help	TurboTax's help topics relating to using the software -- have a search window
	What's New This Year?	Reports the changes in both the tax law and in TurboTax since last year.
	Search for Help On	Opens a topic window with selected topics
	About TurboTax	The people behind the product

FILE

The File menu contains the commands used in handling data files. The New Tax Return option is used to create a new return. When you select this option, the Personal Information Worksheet is displayed. You enter the taxpayer's personal data, i.e. name, address, social security numbers, and other information that is used throughout the return. The Open Tax Return option allows you to load an existing file, identified by its filename, from disk storage. The Save option transfers the data for file specified from RAM to a data disk or directory, i.e., it saves the file, but does not exit the file. A file is closed when you select New Tax Return, or when you select File Exit. The Save As ... command allows you to save the return using another name, perhaps for backup purposes. To save in a different directory, specify the directory as part of the filename, e.g. A:\BillClin.TAX. These commands work in a similar manner in all Microsoft Windows based software.

The Transfer option transfers files created by last year's edition of TurboTax for Windows to the current version. The result is a newly converted file that contains carry over information from the prior year return, including the taxpayer's name and other identifying information. It is a great time saver. However, since this is the first time most of you have used TurboTax, you will not get to use this option. You will have to type all the data from scratch. Life is tough!

The TaxLink Import option is designed with the Quicken or QuickBooks user in mind. If you identify the tax related accounts in your Quicken or QuickBooks accounting software, you can electronically copy that data directly to TurboTax. Thus, if you have recent versions of Quicken or Quickbooks, linking your accounting records to TurboTax is very simple.

The TXF Import option is for those who use older versions of Quicken, QuickBooks, or other accounting software and want to import data into TurboTax. Any accounting software that supports the Tax Exchange Format (TXF) files can also be imported to TurboTax using the Import command. The result is the transfer of data from the accounting software to the tax preparation software, TurboTax. This feature, common to many tax preparation software packages, allows data to be transported between tax prep software. The Remove All Imported Data does just what it says -- it deletes imported data.

FILE PRINT COMMAND

The File Print menu is very user friendly, most of the time. The exception is the unlikely case where your printer is not supported by TurboTax. If your printer is supported, the menu will lead you through the process. Using the Print menu is intuitive and should provide no problems AFTER you have selected your printer. TurboTax will get the basic printer information from Windows. Thus, in most cases, you just confirm the setup. However, if your printer is not directly supported, try to select one that is similar to your printer. Normally you can find one that will produce acceptable output.

When you click on the Print command, you are presented with the Printing dialog box. At the top of the screen the currently selected printer is listed. If this is not the correct printer, i.e. it is not the printer that is currently connected to the PC you are using, you must use the Setup option, at the bottom of the Printing dialog box, to change the selected printer. If you are using this package in a PC lab, check the setup before you print. Things may have changed since you last used the lab. In most college labs, that happens frequently.

The next section prompts you to select the items you want to print. You have three options:

- **Tax Return for Filing** -- If you select this option, the return will be printed with all the schedules and forms required for filing. A suboption, selected by clicking on the adjacent box, will print any itemization statements that were created. These statements provide detailed listings of items that are summed and reported on the various forms and schedules. For most problems, this is the option that you will use.

- **Tax Return for Your Records** -- Use this option to print "the whole thing." In addition to all forms and schedules, you can also print the Itemizations and Smart Worksheets by clicking on the adjacent box. Thus, this option provides you with a paper backup of all of the tax return.

- **Selected Forms** -- If you wish to print only selected forms, schedules, or worksheets, this is the option for you. If you select this option, the box to the right, Choose..., will be highlighted and will allow you to specify the form, schedule, or worksheet that you want to print. Thus, if you wish a second copy of a form, a blank copy of a form to share, or perhaps you need only some forms for you state return, the Selected Forms option allows you to print only what you need.

In the area below, you are provided an opportunity to specify the number of copies you need of your return. Also, you can change the print order from Front to Back to Back to Front. Why? If your printer outputs the printed page face up, you should select Back to Front so that your output will be in order when the print job is complete. If face down, select Front to Back and all will be well.

The final section of the Print screen gives the option to Print, which will print the return; Cancel, which allows you to return to the tax return to do more work; Setup, which moves you to the Printer Setup command where you can modify the printer selected; and Help which opens the Program Help window.

PRINT SETUP

With TurboTax for Windows, the basic setup is handled by Windows. However, there may be some "fine tuning" that you will need to do. The importance of these options varies with the printer that you are using. Recall that printers require special software, called printer drivers, designed just for them. TurboTax assumes that you keep these drivers up-to-date;

thus, be certain that you are using the latest driver for your printer. In general, if you have difficulties with your printer, click on the "Help" button in the Printing dialog box (discussed in the previous section).

LaserJet Series and Compatible

In general, when using HP's LaserJet printers, you should select Portrait orientation, 8.5 by 11 inch or letter size paper, and set the resolution to 300 dpi or higher. No special font cartridges are needed; TurboTax provides its own "soft fonts." Always select "None" in the Cartridge Selection List on the Printer Setup window. If you have problems printing with your laser printer, try selecting the HP III LaserJet printer. Most laser printers will work well with the drivers for this basic laser printer.

IRS PRINTING REQUIRMENTS

The IRS has adapted its printing requirements to recognize the use of personal computers by a large number of people. The requirements are listed for your information.

1. Print the return with black ink on white or cream colored paper, at least 18 pound weight, size 8" x 11" or 8.5"x11". All forms must have a high standard of legibility. Lower quality printers should not be used for the preparation of tax returns. Furthermore, a clean fresh ribbon should be used to insure a dark print.

2. Adjust the page setup to provide a minimum .25" margin on all four sides of the page. Original computer generated forms should be filed, not copies. Vertical spacing should be 6 lines to the inch and horizontal spacing should be 10 characters per inch. All text and numeric data fields must have printer generated underlining.

3. Remove the perforated pin-feed strips on the sides of the paper if you are using continuous-feed paper.

4. Returns must be filed with the forms, schedules and supporting statements assembled in a particular order. Form 1040 always comes first, followed by the forms arranged in order according to the IRS attachment sequence number which is printed in the upper right corner of each form following the year (e.g. "1999 * 09" appears in the upper right corner of the Schedule B). If you need or wish to submit supporting statements with your return, place them behind the required forms and schedules, and arrange them in the same order as the forms and schedules that they support.

5. You are not required to submit itemization details other than what is asked for on the official forms and schedules. If you do wish to submit any of them, arrange them (and any other supporting statements you are filing) in the same order as the forms and schedules they support.

6.   Both spouses, if applicable, must sign the copy of the Form 1040 that you submit to the IRS. Do not submit a return with a photocopied signature.

7.   Use the IRS preprinted mailing label and envelope, if possible.

LISTED FILES

The files listed above the Exit option are the most recent files that you accessed with TurboTax. Thus, if you start one problem, close it and start a second, then go back to the first, you can look at this list of files and open the first directly from the list.

EXIT

Exit allows the user to exit TurboTax and return to the Program Manager or the Desktop with Windows 95/98. If you have made changes to the return which have not been saved, you will be prompted to save these before you exit.

EDIT COMMAND

The Edit commands allow you to change entries. The first option Undo reverses your last command or keystroke thereby allowing you to change the contents of a single field. If you entered an error, you can Undo and return to the point just before you pressed the enter key or click the mouse. If you have not yet entered the data, the option is not available.

You also have the standard editing commands available with all Windows software. Thus, you can Cut, Copy, or Paste one field to another.

You have the option to Override a field that is calculated or transferred from elsewhere. If the field cannot be overridden, the option will appear gray and will display Can't Override. It is not a good idea to override. As you can't fool Mother Nature, TurboTax will rarely treat a transaction in such a way that you will have to override. If you are not careful which field you override, the overridden data can not transfer to other forms correctly. You certainly will have more work to do to check the return if you elect to override. Thus, I urge you to not do it.

The Add Supporting Details option opens an itemization window that lets you enter descriptions and amounts for up to 30 items that will be totaled and put on a single entry line. You can also select the Supporting Details icon or button adjacent to the current field to select or create an itemization schedule for that field. These are very useful when you have a long list of items to enter, for example a list of medical expenses. Note that the Itemization will also do the arithmetic and total the itemized amounts. You can also use these statements to add notes and other supporting statements.

The Mark Estimated option allows you to mark a field as an estimated amount. Thus, you can compute an estimated tax before you have the final numbers. The field that is marked as estimated will be displayed in italic. Also, when you select the Forms errors option, selected by clicking on the yellow triangle with an exclamation point and the words "Forms Errors" icon, the errors listed will include any fields that are estimated. By highlighting the estimated field and double clicking, TurboTax will move you to the estimated field so you can enter the final information. When you move to an estimated field, the option is changed to Unmark Estimated. Thus, when you have all the information, you can move to the estimated field using the Forms Errors option, enter the final information, and then unmark the field with the Edit Unmark Estimated option.

The Options feature allows you limited control over the appearance of the screen. The default is to display all of the features. I suggest that you stay with the default. The features that can be changed are to show or not to show Smart Worksheets, the Tool Bar, Error Alerts, and Status Bar.

The last two options support the editing of tables -- for example a listing of dividends received. The Sort Table option allows you to sort, in alphabetic order for example, a table. The Delete Table Row deletes a row in a table. After deleting rows, you can use the Sort Table option to close the gap. Enough said.

FORMS MENU

Forms Method is built around your use of forms. You select the form that you need to fill out and do it. The Forms Menu brings together the commands that support your use of forms. The first option, "Go To Forms," is active only when you are using EasyStep Interview. It serves the same purpose as the "Go To Forms" icon at the bottom of the EasyStep Interview window, that is you move to the forms. The next option, Open a Form, can be used to access any of the forms available with TurboTax. You can select it from the menu or by using the Forms icon on the Tool Bar. Click on the icon or select the menu option and a listing of the available forms is displayed in a pull-down menu with a scroll bar on the right. Scroll down the listing until you come to the form you need. Double click on the form name and you will move to the form ready to enter the appropriate data.

The option, Show my Return, displays the forms on which you have entered data or to which data has been transferred. If you need to move to a form that you have used previously, the listing displayed by Show my Return will be shorter and provide a faster access to the desired form than that provided by the first option. Unfortunately, there is no icon to support this command.   But, when you click on the Open a Forms icon, the forms window provides you the option to switch between Open a Form and Show my Return. Thus, you are only two clicks away from seeing your forms list.

QuickZoom is a great help in getting around the forms. The command lets you move to a specific form that is attached or linked to the current field. By using the Form 1040 as "command center" and using QuickZoom to move between Form 1040 and the supporting forms, you can efficiently move through a tax return. For example, move the cursor to Line 7 on Form 1040 and double click. TurboTax will take you to the W-2 Worksheet module where you enter the data from your Form W-2, relating to salaries and wages. TurboTax picks up the data from the W-2 Worksheet and places it on the appropriate forms. If you have multiple W-2s, simply click on "Enter New W-2" button and you will be able to create a new W-2 Worksheet. If there is a supporting form for a line on a form, QuickZoom will be active in the Forms Menu. Also, the magnifying glass icon will be attached to the field.

The option Remove <form> is available to delete the current form from your return. Actually, the form itself is a part of TurboTax and will always be available, but this option will delete any data you have entered, and remove the current form from your return. Be careful when you delete a form. If any data is transferred from that form to another, you will be changing the second form also. Normally, this is good. However, just be aware.

Link Field allows you in special circumstances to designate a form to which the amount should be transferred. These circumstances occur when an amount can appear on more than one form. The occurrence of these multiple possibilities for transferring amounts is rare, so do not expect to use this command often.   One example is when you sell depreciable assets; you may have to link a field to Form 6252. Frequently, TurboTax will use this option without your selecting it. It is very user friendly in that regard.

The Select Line option allows you to specify a specific line on the current form and move directly to that line. It can be useful in moving around a tax return.

The Form Errors option displays a listing of fields that contain errors or are marked as estimates.   The command is supported with a button, a small yellow triangle with an exclamation point in its center icon, and the words "Form Errors." You can select any field from the list, move to that form, and correct the error. Some of the errors have no impact on the computation of the tax and are there to provide information used by the IRS or on the state tax return. Thus, an error is frequently the omission of information. This is a command we all need; well maybe not you and I, but all those other people who make errors. Actually, TurboTax keeps track of errors it detects as you go along. When you run the EasyStep Interview option Review, TurboTax uses the Form Errors command to organize these errors, and then moves you to each, one at a time.

The errors are stored continuously as you complete the return, thus, you can go to any form and elect the Find Next Error command (or press F7, Function Key 7,) to move to the line on the form that contains an error. Press F7 a second time and you will move to the next error. When you can move no farther, you have reached the last error on that form. Then move to the next form and repeat the process to correct the errors without directly using the Review feature.

The New, Next, and Previous Copy command helps you to move among the various information forms you receive, such as W-2s, 1099's, etc. The New Copy allows you to create a new form. The Magnify Form command is similar to the ZOOM command in most Windows software. The command will enlarge the screen and make the data easier to read. The default is 100 percent; keep it.

EASYSTEP MENU

The EasyStep menu option connects Forms Method and EasyStep Interview. You can use this menu option to move to any one of the EasyStep Interview nine steps. Thus, you are able to use the convenience of EasyStep Interview to help you complete a particularly difficult form and then return to Forms Method to complete the remainder of the return. To return to the Form, click on the Go to Forms ... button in the lower right-hand corner of the EasyStep Interview screen. (You would first have to click on the "Show Tax Form" button if the tax form is not shown in the lower portion of the screen.) Refer to Chapter 3 for a more in depth look at EasyStep Interview.

The Back to Interview option will move you from Forms Method to where you left off in EasyStep Interview. When you come to a difficult area of a tax return, you can select EasyStep Interview. For example, if you are having trouble deciding how to handle a distribution from an IRA, you could enter EasyStep Interview, scroll to Retirement, and then select Pension/IRA Distributions. EasyStep Interview will walk you through reporting the IRA distribution. Then, you can return to the forms by clicking on the "Go to Forms..." button in the lower right corner of the EasyStep Interview screen.

EasyStep Interview uses a dialog box to display its questions and give space for your answers. You supply the information which is then transferred to the appropriate areas of the actual return that is shown in the bottom window on the screen. Normally, you do not enter information directly onto the forms while using the Interview. The program does it for you. As you progress through the questions, these forms are automatically updated. A check is placed next to each sub-topic in the list of items after it has been completed.

Recall from Chapter 3, a portion of the current form will be displayed in the bottom half of the screen while you are using EasyStep Interview. While you normally do not enter data directly on the form, you do have the option of making changes directly on the form. Thus, the form is live in the sense that you can edit it. You are encouraged to only edit the form and not stay in EasyStep Interview to enter data on forms. Use Forms Method if that is your preferred method. If the data in the field is transferred from another form or worksheet, you will not be able to make changes on that field. You will have to make the changes at the source.

As you move through the Interview, you will notice some of the words in the questions are light blue. You can move your mouse pointer to these words and click on the words to open TurboTax on-screen Help to view a definition or explanation of the tax term.

Having the ability of moving between the user friendly EasyStep Interview and the efficient Forms Method allows the user to have the best of both worlds. Do not hesitate to use these features. They are in the program to help you complete the return.

TOOLS MENU

The Tools Menu collects the various commands that provide you with convenient tools to help you complete your tax return. The first, My Tax Data opens a window listing all of your entries and their respective tax forms and lines. It is a listing of all the information that you entered in completing the tax return. You can move the cursor to any line and double click to move to the highlighted form and line. Once there, you can edit the line and correct any error. Thus, if you misspelled the abbreviation for Virginia, you can scan the "What you entered" column, highlight the error, select "Go to Form," and make your correction.

The Final Review option opens the Review step of EasyStep Interview and performs a review of your tax return. The option will find the errors and then lead you to each one with an opportunity to correct each error.

The Topic Search option helps you find where to report those unusual items of income and expense that occur in most tax returns. Topic Search works like most search options in Windows based software. Selecting the Topic Search option opens a box with two response boxes. In the first, you enter description of the transaction. TurboTax will search the listing of topics and display those that match your request in the second response box. You select the one you want and click on the "Display Topic" button at the bottom of the dialog box. TurboTax takes you to the appropriate EasyStep Interview question for this topic.

The Calculator option is very useful. This command opens an on-the-screen calculator with the basic arithmetical functions. In addition, the calculator has a "paste" feature that will put the total shown on the calculator in the current empty field. Data entry is always better if it can be done by the computer.

The Tax Summary tool will display on the screen a brief summary of your tax return. It lists the major items such as the total gross income, adjusted gross income, taxable income, taxes, tax withheld and tax due or refund due. You can select the option before and after entering a transaction to see the marginal impact of one specific transaction.

The What-if Worksheet allows you to compare the current tax return with three alternatives. The worksheet supports copying the current tax return to the other columns. Then you can make changes to the columns by scrolling to the cell and editing the entry. Thus, you can compare a total of four alternatives at one time. Very useful when you do basic tax planning.

The History Worksheet is useful if you have the data. To have the history worksheet automatically created, you must have used TurboTax in the previous year and have a carryover data file that is created when you import your return to the current year. The worksheet reports a total of five years of taxes, the three previous years, the current year and the next year. If this is the first year you have used TurboTax, you can enter the data in each cell by referring to your prior years returns. A five-year summary of your tax returns is very useful in tax planning.

The Tax Graphs option will display the current year's tax summary in four graphs. One of the graphs shows you how the Federal government spent your tax dollars.

WINDOW MENU

The Window Menu offers three methods of viewing open windows, allows you to quickly close all open windows, and lists each active form and window. These options are common to all Windows software.

Tile arranges all open windows in smaller sizes to fit next to each other on the desktop.

Cascade causes all open windows to overlap so that each title bar is visible. This is the default display. You can of course override this by clicking the right most arrow head on an active form to display the form on the entire screen.

Arrange Icons rearranges the form icons in the bottom left area of your screen so that they are evenly spaced and do not overlap.

Close Windows closes the current window without affecting any other opened windows. The Close All Windows closes all the opened windows but does not close TurboTax. To leave TurboTax, you must use the File Exit command.

The bottom portion of the Window Menu lists the windows that are currently open in TurboTax. Selecting a window from this list (by double clicking) lets you switch between windows. Thus, you can move between the open windows very easily using this option.

HELP MENU

The Help menu allows you to select from the various sources of help available with TurboTax. It is an additional way to access all of the help features described earlier, such as descriptions of tax rules, official IRS instructions, frequently asked questions, etc.

TURBOTAX ICONS FOR FORMS METHOD

The Tool Bar displayed across the top of the screen lists the most commonly used commands (e.g., File, Edit, etc.). Below the Tool Bar are seven icons and buttons that are only displayed when Forms Method is selected. Each is discussed briefly.

```
TurboTax - [Form 1040: Individual Tax Return]
  File   Edit   View   Forms   EasyStep   Tools   Online   Window   Help
  Save  |  Print  | Open a Form | Form Errors | Final Review | Search |     Help
   1        2          3             4             5            6           7
```

1.   The first icon is the image of a floppy disk and the word "Save." Clicking the icon will save the current file to the current disk -- File Save is the command being used.

2.   The second icon is a printer. It is used to print forms from your current tax return.

3.   The next icon is the Forms icon, three small forms and the words "Open a Form." It displays the Form Selection Menu that lists all available forms, schedules, or worksheets. You will use this option to select the required form. When you enter the Form Selection Menu, you will have the option of listing all forms, or only those that relate to the current tax return. The command being used is the Forms command, Open a Form option.

4.   The fourth icon is a small yellow triangle with an exclamation point in the middle and the words "Form Errors." This icon will display a listing of errors identified by the Final Review feature of TurboTax. You can scroll through the listing and move to the one you are ready to correct. The command used is the Forms command, Form Errors option.

5.   The fifth icon is "Final Review." This button will execute TurboTax review of the tax return and identify those errors listed by the Form Errors icon. The command used is the Tools command, Final Review option.

6.   The next icon is the Search button. This button activates the Tools command, Topics List Search option. The command allows you to search from an indexed listing of common tax transactions and receive more information as to the proper treatment of that transaction.

7.   The last icon is ?Help, the icon that activates the TurboTax Help menu. There you will have your choice of three types of help: Tax Help, Government (IRS) Instructions, and Program Help. The help given is for the current field; that is referred to as "context sensitive." The help in TurboTax is useful; expect to use it.

This completes the list of icons on the Tool Bar. You will save time clicking on the icon rather than going to the command menus and selecting the commands. But both ways will get the job done. And that is the important point.

TURBOTAX WORKSHEETS

TurboTax builds the tax return from a foundation of Forms and Schedules that are official IRS documents. To these, TurboTax adds a variety of worksheets designed to facilitate the entry of tax data. Included are "smart worksheets" which are imposed on some of the IRS's forms to aid data entry for that form, and interactive worksheets designed to support complicated transactions, such as the depreciation worksheet -- called the Asset Entry Worksheet. Figure 4-3 lists some of the worksheets used by TurboTax. The worksheets are designed to focus on key information required to correctly report complicated tax transactions. If you do not complete the worksheet, you will have to use the Override command to enter the correct tax data. It easier to use the worksheets. In addition, you might learn some tax law by using the worksheet.

Smart Worksheets

TurboTax has created *Smart Worksheets* to aid you in entering data. Rather than using a separate worksheet to help you determine the appropriate total, you can use the shorter smart worksheets that are embedded in the form. These worksheets will appear on the screen but will not be printed when the form itself is printed. They are not a part of the official IRS form, rather simply an added space to report the information required by the form. While you can turn off the display of the Smart Worksheets using the Edit Options command, I urge you not to do so. The smart worksheets are there for your convenience. Use them.

Figure 4-3 TurboTax Worksheets	
Form 1040	Personal Information Worksheet, Which Forms to complete, Form W-2: Wage & Tax Statement, Form 1099-Misc Worksheet, Form 1099-R: Pension Distributions, Line 7 Statement, State Tax Refund Worksheet, IRA, Keogh, SEP Contribution Worksheet, Social Security Income Worksheet, Other Income Worksheet, Tax Payments Worksheet, Additional Dependents Statement
Schedule A	Medical Expenses Worksheet, Tax & Interest Deduction Statement, Charitable Contributions Statement, Miscellaneous Itemized Deductions Statement, Itemized Deductions Worksheet
Schedule B	Interest Income Statement, Additional Interest Income Statement, Dividend Income Statement, Additional Dividend Income Statement, Seller-Financed Mortgage Interest Statement.
Schedule D	Additional Capital Gains & Losses Statement, Worksheets for Schedule D
Schedule E	Schedule K-1 Worksheet--Partnership, Schedule K-1 Worksheet--S Corporations, Schedule K-1 Worksheet--Estates & Trusts, Sch E Partnerships & S Corps Report, Sch E:
Schedule EIC	Earned Income Credit Worksheet, Earned Income Worksheet
Schedule R	Sch R AMT Limit Worksheet
Form 4562	Sec 179 Expense Report
Form 8582	Modified AGI Worksheet, Passive Activities Worksheet 1, Passive Activities Worksheet 2, Passive Activities Worksheet 3,4,5,6,Passive Activities Worksheet 1-AMT, Passive Activities Worksheet 2-AMT, 3-AMT,4-AMT,5-AMT,6-AMT
Federal Income Tax Carryover Worksheet	

Data Entry Worksheets

Several of the worksheets are full page worksheets that are designed to aid you in entering data. To use these worksheets enter the detailed tax data as prompted by the worksheet. Then TurboTax takes over and the individual items are totaled, and the totals are transferred by TurboTax to the appropriate line and form. For example, many taxpayers have income from wages or salaries and receive a Form W-2 from their employer. TurboTax has provided a worksheet, called the "Form W-2 Wage & Tax Statement," to summarize W-2 forms.

TurboTax for Windows allows ten W-2's, or "copies" of W-2's per taxpayer.   The worksheet mirrors the actual form W-2 received by the taxpayer, thus, the required data can be entered exactly as seen on the W-2. Double clicking on Line 7 of the Form 1040, takes you to the Form W-2 Worksheet. The first step in using the W-2 Worksheet is to enter the employer's name. When you arrive at the W-2 Worksheet, you should note the box at the top of the worksheet that is used to identify the W-2 as for the Spouse or not. The spouse could be either the Husband or the Wife, as long as you are consistent. The W-2 Worksheet asks for the "Control Number." The number is required for electronic filing. Also it is on the W-2, so it is on the worksheet. It has no impact on your tax liability, thus you can skip it if you desire or if the information is not available (as is the case in most of the problems in this manual.) After you have entered all the information from the W-2's, TurboTax will summarize all W-2's and transfer the totals to Line 7 on Form 1040. While you can use the Override command and enter the W-2 amounts directly on Line 7 and other applicable lines, you will find it easier to use the W-2 Worksheet.

The most common way of moving to supporting worksheets or forms is to double click (*QuickZoom*) on the line supported. In addition, you can select the worksheet or form from the Open Form window. You can access this menu by clicking on the Forms icon on the Tool Bar. If you use the EasyStep Interview approach, TurboTax will select the appropriate worksheet and ask the correct questions, prompting you to enter the required data.

Asset Entry Worksheet

The Asset Entry Worksheet is used to calculate deductions for assets used in a trade or business or held for production of income. This is a very important worksheet and should be used for ALL depreciation calculations. The worksheet is very flexible and complete. It will handle substantially all problems with computing depreciation. I urge you to rely on the worksheet. A copy of the worksheet follows on the next two pages. Note that there is a special worksheet for computing depreciation on cars and trucks. It should be used for all computations relating to the use of cars or trucks in a business.

In TurboTax all depreciation related entries (other than those for cars and trucks) are made in the Asset Entry Worksheet. As with all forms in TurboTax for Windows, when you use Forms Method you start with the field where the final number is reported and *QuickZoom* to the supporting worksheet. Thus, you start by moving the pointer to the field where the depreciation expense is reported, for example Line 13 on Schedule C.   Then you QuickZoom (double click) to access the Asset Entry Worksheet. While the IRS uses Form 4562 to report all depreciation expenses, TurboTax takes care of that by transferring the amounts from the worksheet to the appropriate forms. The only place you need to make an entry is on the Asset Entry Worksheet or its first cousin, the Car and Truck Expenses Worksheet which is used for all vehicles.

The Asset Entry Worksheet leads you through the relevant factors that determine the method and amount of depreciation for the various types of assets. The Asset Entry Worksheet makes assumptions based upon your answers. Thus, you may need only answer a few of the questions before TurboTax is able to determine the amount of depreciation for your asset. After you have entered the information in the General Asset Information and Type of Asset sections of the worksheet, frequently the remainder of the worksheet will be automatically computed. Of course you should check page 2 of the worksheet to be certain it is completed. Take a moment to look at the Asset Entry Worksheet on the following pages; it will help you understand the procedure.

The first few times you use the worksheet you need to read carefully. The Asset Entry Worksheet is also used to report the disposition of assets and it includes questions relating to such dispositions. When you record an asset that is purchased in the current year, these questions do not apply. Just ignore them and all will be fine.

If the terms on the Asset Entry Worksheet are not familiar to you, I suggest that you review the Tax Help to investigate the meaning of the terms. Simply move the cursor to the field you have a question about and click on the *Help* icon. Also, I will remind you that you have a textbook that explains how the tax system determines depreciation or cost recovery allowances. It is also useful to you.

NOTE ABOUT SECTION 179

Section 179 allows taxpayers to expense up to $19,000 (in 1999, more in later years) of tangible personal property used in a trade or business. If the taxpayer is engaged in more than one trade or business (i.e. the taxpayer has more than one Schedule C), each Schedule C must be supported by a different Form 4562. However, TurboTax will transfer ALL SECTION 179 amounts from either the Asset Entry Worksheet or the Car and Truck Expenses Worksheet to the Section 179 Expense Report. From there the amounts are summarized and transferred to Form 4562 if you have only one activity or to Form 4562: Section 179 Limitation, if you have more than one activity. This is the Form 4562 used to report the total Section 179 deduction. If all of your Section 179 deduction applies to one activity, a regular Form 4562 will report all information relating to depreciation and Section 179 expense on the same Form 4562. If you have more than one activity that incurs Section 179 expenses, the limit is determined on Form 4562: Section 179 Limitation and then you have to allocate the total Section 179 allowable deduction to the various Forms 4562. To do so you will have to **Override** the amount on Line 12 of the various Forms 4562 and enter the allocated amount. Of course the total Section 179 expense reported on the various lines 12 can not exceed the total allowable as determined on Form 4562: Section 179 Limitation. This form (Form 4562: Section 179 Limitation) is not printed as a part of the tax return.

A second limit of Section 179 is the taxable income from all trades or businesses. TurboTax computes this amount and enters the total business income on the taxable income limit line, Line 11 of Form 4562. In addition, the overall limit of $19,000 is reduced by the purchase of qualifying assets in excess of $200,000, based upon the total of all transactions incurred by the taxpayer during the year. TurboTax applies the limit on Form 4562, not on the Asset Entry Worksheet. Thus, when you complete the worksheet, the amount of Section 179 deduction may exceed $19,000. When you view Form 4562, you will note that the limit has been applied.

Name(s) Shown on Return	Social Security Number
Larry Sample	234-87-5643

Activity: Sch C

Asset Information   (For vehicles, use the Car and Truck Expenses Worksheet)

1   Description of asset .... Computer   Example: Laser printer

2   Date placed in service .... 06/10/99   Example: 06/15/99

3   Enter the total cost when asset was acquired .   3,500.   Include land for asset type I, J or M

4   Type of asset .... A - Computer

5   Percentage of business use .... 100.00 %   Range: 1.00 to 100.00
If blank, 100.00% is used.
Applicable for asset type A - G, P.

6   Enter the amount of Sec 179 expense elected   0.   Subject to limitation. See Tax Help.

7   Total amount of land included in the cost .....   0.   Applicable for asset type I, J or M
If blank, prior depreciation from
Asset Life History is used.

8   Prior depreciation ....   0.   Required if asset was sold.

9   **Depreciation deduction** ....   700.

If blank, prior depreciation from
Asset Life History is used.

10   AMT prior depreciation ....   0.   Required if asset was sold.

11   AMT depreciation deduction ....   525.

12   AMT adjustment/preference ....   175.   See Tax Help for computation

13   **QuickZoom** to Asset Life History ....

14   If a computer or peripheral equipment (asset type A), was asset
used exclusively at your regular business establishment? .... ☐ Yes ☒ No

15   If video, photo, or phono equipment (asset type B),
was asset used exclusively at your regular business establishment,
or in connection with your principal trade or business? .... ☐ Yes ☐ No

16   If rental appliances, carpeting, or furniture (asset type F), have you
amended your 1998 tax return or filed Form 3115 to change
the recovery period to 5 years? .... ☐ Yes ☐ No

17   Enter the IRC section under which you amortize
the cost of intangibles (asset type L) ....

18   Home Office copy number for home office (asset type M) or
home office improvement (asset type N) ....

Dispositions   Complete this part only if you sold, abandoned, or otherwise disposed
of this asset in 1999.

19   Date sold, given away,
     or abandoned in 1999 .... _____   Example: 12/01/99
20   Asset sales price .... _____   Enter business portion only
21   Asset expense of sale .... _____   Enter business portion only
22   Property type .... _____

23   Land sales price .... _____   Enter business portion only
24   Land expense of sale .... _____   Enter business portion only

25   If Section 1250:
   a   Additional depreciation after 1975 .... _____
   b   Applicable percentage .... _____ %
   c   Additional depreciation after 1969 and before 1976 .... _____

26   Double click to link sale to Form 6252 .... _____

27   Basis for gain or loss, if different from ln 3 .... _____   Enter 100% of basis
28   Basis for AMT gain or loss, if diff from ln 48 .. _____   Enter 100% of basis

29   Gain or loss .... _____
30   AMT gain or loss .... _____
31   Part of Form 4797 that gain or loss carries to .... _____
32   Land gain or loss (if separate) .... _____   Only applies if line 23 is entered
33   Part of Form 4797 that land gain or loss carries to (if separate) .... _____
34   Home office depreciation after May 6, 1997 ... _____   See Tax Help

Detail Asset Information   This section is calculated for most assets from the data above.
Use Find Next Error feature to check for any required entries.

#						
35	Listed property?	X	Yes		No	See Tax Help
36	Subject to automobile limitations?		Yes	X	No	
37	Electric Passenger Vehicle?		Yes	X	No	
38	Eligible Section 179 property?		Yes	X	No	Applies to current year assets only
39	Use IRS tables for MACRS property?		Yes	X	No	

Regular Depreciation
40   Depreciation Type .... MACRS   _____
41   Asset class 5   _____
42   Depreciation Method .... 200DB   _____
43   MACRS convention .... HY   _____
44   **QuickZoom** to set 1999 convention .... ████████
45   Recovery period .... _____ 5.0
46   Year of depreciation .... _____ 1
47   Depreciable basis .... _____ 3,500.   See Tax Help for computation

Alternative Minimum Tax Depreciation
48   AMT basis, if different from line 3 .... _____
49   If placed in service before 1987, is asset ...... _____
50   AMT depreciation method .... 150DB   _____
51   AMT recovery period .... _____ 5.0
52   AMT depreciable basis .... _____ 3,500.

In summary, the Asset Entry Worksheet is flexible and thorough. It is recommended that you use it in all cases where the taxpayer has depreciation expenses. The worksheet is flexible enough to correctly compute depreciation for the current year even if you placed the asset in service in an earlier year. The codes used to identify the correct method are complicated, but if you use the worksheet from the start, TurboTax will enter the correct codes for you. That way, it is simple.

INCOME FROM PARTNERSHIPS and S CORPORATIONS

Certain legal entities do not pay income tax directly. These entities pass their income and deductions to their owners and the owners pay the tax. These entities are referred to as "flowthrough entities." Trusts, Estates, Partnerships and S Corporations are the common examples of flowthrough entities. The owners receive a copy of a Schedule K-1 that reports their share of the income, expenses and other tax items from the flowthrough entity.

TurboTax treats the Schedules K-1 in the same manner that Forms W-2 are handled. Thus, the various K-1s (limit of ten) are summarized and reported on the appropriate form. Since the K-1s the taxpayer receives will be substantially identical to the Schedule K-1 worksheets, it is a simple task to enter the amounts in the appropriate places. You need to pay particular attention to the General Information and Activity Information sections at the top of the worksheet. It is here that you will identify if the partnership interest is owned by the taxpayer, the spouse or jointly. Also, the Activity Information is essential in determining whether or not the activity should be treated as passive activity. The assumption is that the activity **is** passive, thus you enter an X (i.e. click on the mouse) if the activity is NOT PASSIVE. For real estate activities, you must indicate the level of participation -- material or active. Also, you must indicate if the activity is a qualified low-income housing activity. This information is used in applying and reporting the passive activities of the taxpayer. It is important. If you are uncertain of the terms, use the *Help* button.

PASSIVE ACTIVITIES

If you have gains or losses from passive activities (including prior year disallowed losses), you must file Form 8582. (There are some exceptions that are indicated on the form.) Form 8582 is used to calculate the amount of loss from passive activities that is allowed on your tax return. TurboTax prepares Form 8582 automatically, that is all entries on Form 8582 are based on information from the Passive Activity Worksheets and other forms in your tax return. There are six passive activity worksheets which are used to limit passive activity losses on an activity-by-activity basis.

The flow of information to the Passive Activity Worksheets is controlled by the information you provide on other tax forms. As noted above, the key questions that appear on the Schedule K-1s and other forms are:

1.   Check if Material Participation -- If yes then the ordinary income or loss from trade or business activities are not passive activities; otherwise, they are included as passive activities and summarized on the Passive Activities Worksheets that are summarized on Form 8582.

2.   Check if Active Participation in the operation of the activity -- If you check here, the real estate activities up to the applicable limits are not considered passive.

3.   Check if Complete Disposition -- Checking indicates that you have disposed of the property and are entitled to all current and deferred losses. Not checking indicates that you still own the property and are therefore still subject to the passive activity loss limitations.

Careful consideration of your answers to these questions on the various forms will insure you that Form 8582 will be completed for all current passive activities. The forms, schedules and worksheets that will transfer amounts to the Passive Activity Loss Worksheets are listed below for your information.

*   Schedules C, E, and F
*   Form 6252, Installment Sales
*   K-1 Worksheets for Partnerships, S Corporations, and Estates and Trusts
*   Worksheet for Federal Income Tax Carryover Data

The major problem you will have is the addition of carryover information that is not included on the Worksheet for Federal Income Tax Carryover Data. If you used TurboTax in the prior year, the File Transfer option will correctly add any carryover amounts to the carryover worksheet and from there to the various schedules that report the activity. However, if this is the first year that you have used TurboTax, the appropriate information relating to the passive loss carryovers must be added to this year's return. Carryovers can be added to the activity's schedule, Schedule C, K-1 Worksheet, at the end of the worksheet, etc. If you are using EasyStep Interview, it will walk you through the appropriate questions. If you get stuck using Forms Method, select EasyStep Interview and let TurboTax do the work. You can press F1 along the way to display information to help you answer the questions. These help screens are useful; use them.

The bottom-line is that if you correctly answer the required questions, TurboTax will complete Form 8582 for current year's transactions. If there are no carryovers, that's it. If you have carryovers, they must be correctly entered on either the K-1 worksheet or other activity worksheet.

SELF-EMPLOYMENT INCOME

Self-employment income from partnerships is reported on K-1s. In entering the income on the K-1 worksheets, you must be certain to enter the income on line 15a and on line 15b or 15c in order to correctly compute the Self-employment tax. Self-employment income from sole proprietorships is transferred from Schedule C to the appropriate line on Schedule SE. TurboTax does the work for you. If you reported the amounts correctly, the self-employment income and related tax will be correctly computed.

ALTERNATIVE MINIMUM TAX

Form 6251 must be completed to report all amounts that may result in an Alternative Minimum Tax. TurboTax calculates much of the form automatically, although you may need to OVERRIDE certain lines on Form 6251 if your tax situation involves an exception or a special case. One type of special case is the occurrence of a loss from an activity where the taxpayer is not at-risk. TurboTax does not check if an asset was used in an activity for which you are not at-risk. Thus, you may be required to use the OVERRIDE option to adjust the loss amount if you are not at-risk. You may have to make some entries for amounts not picked up by the program (i.e. those fields on Form 6251 that are "Enter Amount" fields).

The major point is that TurboTax is going to correctly transfer the required amounts from other forms to Form 6251. For those situations where there are questions about how to report AMT related transactions, use EasyStep Interview to get help. For most taxpayers, you will only have to explain the tax to the taxpayer. TurboTax can figure it out.

PENALTY FOR UNDERPAYMENT OF ESTIMATED TAX

TurboTax will compute the penalty for underpayment of estimated tax reported on Form 2210. The computation is based upon payment amounts you entered on the W-2 Worksheets, Carryover Worksheet, and the Form 1040. The program also uses the information you enter on Form 2210. TurboTax and the IRS assume that all estimated tax payment amounts were equal over the year. If they were not, you have to check the appropriate box on Form 2210 and use the OVERRIDE command to enter the Quarterly amounts. The IRS encourages that you do not file Form 2210. Instead the IRS will compute the penalty and bill the taxpayer. As noted on Form 2210 there are four exceptions. If you are required to file Form 2210, TurboTax will support its preparation. As a real world warning, in the past, the IRS has been notorious for computing unusual amounts as penalty taxes. This is one area of tax where "To err is human. To really foul things up requires an IRS computer." Fortunately, TurboTax does better.

WHERE CAN YOU GET MORE SUPPORT?

If after reading this manual, looking at all of the Help features, seeking help on the TurboTax web site (www.turbotax.com), and asking your friend in the course, you still are having trouble using TurboTax, there is support straight from trained TurboTax support personnel. See page 5-3 for telephone numbers and related information. Another source of help is the Intuit Inc. web page. The URL is

http://www.intuit.com

Part of this web page is Frequently Asked Questions where you can get substantial information about TurboTax. There is an e-mail link for you to ask questions directly to the support staff. They will answer by e-mail also.

When you call, be certain that you know what type of PC you are using, the type of printer, disk drives, processor, and that you know what error messages you received if any. The people in the installation group are very patient, but they need this information if they are to be able to help you solve the problem. It is also extremely helpful if you can be sitting at your PC, with the PC up and running when you call. For more information about the customer service available from Intuit Inc., also look at the next chapter.

CONCLUDING COMMENTS

All the command options available with TurboTax for Windows are discussed above. As stated along the way, TurboTax can help you as a last resort, but will not make tax decisions for you. You will need to study the tax law in order to know how to treat the various transactions that occur during a normal year. The program is forms-oriented and provides help in identifying the forms that you need for certain transactions. You will still need to summarize the transactions for the year and to be aware of which transactions to pursue further.

As with any software, you need to use it to learn it. In Chapter 6 you are provided with practice problems and some solutions. In addition, the first problem gives you a step-by-step walk through the use of TurboTax. Regardless of your level of knowledge about using the personal computer, I assure you that you can use TurboTax to prepare a tax return.

Good luck!

CHAPTER 5

CUSTOMER SERVICE FROM TURBOTAX

TurboTax software included with this manual is the version that is distributed by Intuit Inc. for personal use. All TurboTax users, including students and faculty, are eligible to obtain support from experts at Intuit Inc. Support is available if difficulties are encountered while installing or using TurboTax and the user is unable to rectify the situation <u>after</u> reading this manual and searching the TurboTax Help options. The purpose of this chapter is to identify Intuit Inc. customer services. Note, however, that you should <u>not</u> rely on TurboTax support to answer questions concerning tax law arising from tax course assignments.

If you have difficulty using TurboTax

First, don't panic. Think through the steps you have just followed. There are resources available to help you. If there is an error message on your screen, write it on a sheet of paper for later reference.

Steps for solving TurboTax technical difficulties are as follows:

1. Consult this manual, Program Help, and the READ1040 file, discussed in Chapter 2.

2. Confirm that your computer conforms to the system requirements discussed in Chapter 2.

3.   If you are still having trouble, connect to the Intuit Inc. web site (www.intuit.com) or call the Intuit Inc. toll-free automated technical support services at 1-800-685-7369.

TurboTax Web site http://www.turbotax.com

TurboTax technical support is available from the World Wide Web 24 hours a day.   The TurboTax Web site is constantly updated and offers:

1.   Technical support information and answers to frequently asked questions

2.   Downloadable program updates

3.   Late-breaking tax and product news

4.   TurboTax federal and state product information

5.   Downloadable TurboTax State software

Automated technical support (800) 685-7369

Toll-free automated technical support (ATS) provides recordings of frequently asked questions, technical support tips, late-breaking news about TurboTax, and product updates. Information is constantly updated.

To use ATS, you need a touch-tone telephone, a pen or pencil, and a piece of paper.

1.   ATS asks you a series of questions to which you respond by pressing telephone keys.

2.   Based on information you provide, ATS provides possible solutions

3.   You can save your ATS session, then return to it after you try the proposed solution

    If you save your ATS session (ATS tells you how), ATS provides a case number. Write down the case number. The next time you call, enter the case number and ATS retrieves the session in progress; that way you don't have to start your session over at the beginning.

Tip   If you have access to a fax machine or fax modem, you can have recorded ATS information sent to you by fax. ATS tells you how.

Technical support representatives (520) 901-3240

Note: Free technical support is only available for initial installation, electronic filing problems, printing problems, or product defects.

Regular Hours: Monday through Friday, 5:00 a.m. to 5:00 p.m., Pacific time

Extended Hours: January 3, 2000 through April 17, 2000
   Monday - Friday, 5:00 p.m. to 8:00 p.m., Pacific time
   Saturday, 8:00 a.m. to 8:00 p.m., Pacific time
   Sunday, 8:00 a.m. to 6:00 p.m., Pacific time

During extended hours, Technical Support costs $1.95 per minute.

Fax service (800) 766-5034

If you have a fax machine or a fax modem, use Intuit Inc.'s toll-free Fax service for frequently asked questions, technical support tips, late-breaking news about TurboTax, and product updates. Fax documents are constantly updated.

Before you call, write down your area code and fax number and have them in front of you.

1.   **Call (800) 766-5034.**
     TaxFax gives you instructions on how to choose either a particular document that applies to your situation or a catalog that lists all available document topics.

2.   **At the prompt, choose to receive either a particular document or the catalog of documents.**
     You can request up to three documents at a time.

3.   **At the prompt, enter your fax number and phone number.**
     Remain on the line while the system processes your request. The line automatically disconnects, and the requested documents are faxed to you, usually within minutes of your call. If you do not receive your documents within four hours of your call, call and make your request again.

CHAPTER 6

TAX RETURN PROBLEMS

The purpose of this chapter is to provide tax return homework problems for your use in learning TurboTax. The problems give you the opportunity to work with most of the tax forms available with TurboTax. You may encounter some transactions that have not been covered in your tax course. Welcome to the real world. One of the strengths of TurboTax is its Help features, both Tax Help and Program Help. You are encouraged to use Help features while you are preparing returns.

Names and other tax data in all problems are fictitious. Any resemblance to specific individuals is purely coincidental.

Tax forms occasionally ask questions that are designed to aid in the audit of a wide variety of transactions. Accordingly, several questions apply in only limited circumstances. If the problem information does not address one of the questions, leave the answer blank. Make no entry of any kind unless instructed otherwise by your professor. The risk in guessing at such entries is that you may mark a transaction for special treatment by TurboTax.

Complete solutions are provided for Problems 1 and 2. Problem 1 is followed by step-by-step instructions to complete the problem, thereby providing a guided tour of TurboTax. These solutions were prepared using the same version of the software that is included with this manual.

If you want to work with tax return homework problems in addition (or instead of) the problems in this chapter, consider looking in the end-of-chapter problems of your tax textbook. As with any complex task, the more practice you have, the more skilled you will become. Thus, you are encouraged to work as many tax return problems as your schedule permits.

PROBLEM 1 Mary Brown

Objective: Sample problem and solution. Wage income and interest income.

Mary Brown is an accounting major at the University of Michigan who is single and works part-time in the summer as a cashier for the Michigan House, the premier restaurant in Acme. Mary was born September 20, 1978. She presents you with the following information:

Social security number	345-23-4567
Address	345 Florida Ave., Acme, MI 49610
Home telephone number	313-555-5555
Employer	Michigan House, One Main Street, employer number 65-76543256
Wages on Form W-2	$ 4,150
Federal income taxes withheld	$ 100
State income taxes W/H	$ 0
Social security taxes	$ 257
Medicare taxes	$ 60

In addition, Mary received $680 in interest income from the Bank of Acme. Mary has no interest from any other accounts.

Mary lived at home during the summer. Her parents provide more than 85 percent of her support throughout the year. If allowable, Mary's parents plan to claim her as a dependent. Mary supports the Presidential Election Campaign Fund and does want $3 to go to that fund.

REQUIRED: Complete Mary's federal income tax return.

STEP-BY-STEP SOLUTION

The following pages provide a step-by-step solution of this problem using EasyStep Interview.

STEP 1: Load TurboTax.

Refer to the installation procedures in Chapter 2. With Windows 95/98, click on the Start button, move the mouse pointer to "Programs," and then to the TurboTax for Windows 1999, and then to the TurboTax icon titled "1999 TurboTax for Windows." Click to load TurboTax. You are immediately welcomed and invited to click on the "Let's get started" button.

STEP 2: Start EasyStep Interview

After being welcomed and invited to click on the "Let's Get Started" button, you have the option to view various screens containing background information. You have the opportunity to load tax information from your last year's tax return. For this and other tax return problems in this chapter (and in most textbook problems), there is not a prior year's return available. Thus, click on the "Start My Return" button and then the "Continue" button. Since you are not tranferring data from last year's tax return or other programs, click on the "Skip transfer" button and the "Skip import" button when you see them. Continue to click on the appropriate buttons to proceed to the "Your Filing Status" screen - Figure 6-1, below. This is where you begin to input information to TurboTax.

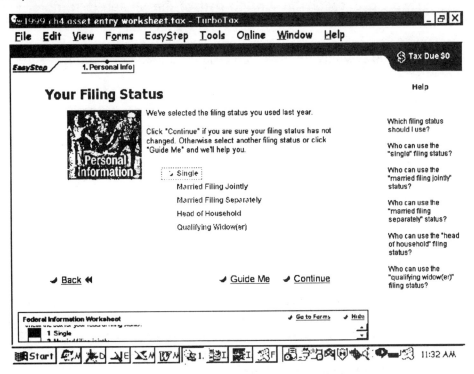

Figure 6-1 The first EasyStep Interview screen

The first piece of information provided to TurboTax is marital status. Since Mary is single, click on the first "radio button," titled "single." Click on the blue "Continue" button to proceed.

STEP 3: Continue answering Interview questions

The second interview screen requests the taxpayer's name, birthdate and social security number. Enter this information for Mary. When entering birthdays, you must enter in the form mm/dd/yy. You can enter the slashes but TurboTax will include them automatically if you do not. If you have a single-digit month or day, you must precede with the number with a zero. Thus, September 20, 1978 is entered as 092078 and appears as 09/20/78 after it is entered.

Why does TurboTax ask for your birth date and other information seemingly unrelated to tax return preparation? The reason is that many state returns require it. Your birthday is important so TurboTax can determine if you are over 65, or over 25 for the Earned Income Credit.

Notice that you will see the information you enter appear on the appropriate lines on the tax return form in the window at the bottom of the screen. Viewing the forms in this manner will help you learn how they are prepared and how one form relates to others. Moreover, you can edit and/or add information in the bottom part of the screen by clicking on an item. Thus, an alternative to answering questions in the top part of the screen is to enter information directly on the forms in the bottom half of the screen.

The next screen allows you to verify the taxpayer's name and social security. After doing so, click on the Continue button.

Now comes a series of questions. When you do not have the requested information, leave it blank. If you are not certain of the answer, take the default answer — the one with the light, dotted line on the button. EasyStep Interview will prompt you to save your file from time to time. You should do so.

Mailing address and home phone

Information about your state

Occupation and work phone

Someone's Dependent: Tax knowledge is necessary here. Very briefly, Mary meets the relationship test, gross income test (student exception); support test (car counts but scholarship does not count); joint return test, and residency test. Thus, Mary can be claimed as someone's dependent. If you were not certain, you could click on Help, and TurboTax would give you the tax law.

Military: No

Permanently disabled: No

Legally blind: No

Taxpayer died: No

Contribute $3 of tax to the Presidential Election Campaign Fund: Yes

Dependents: None (click on "Skip Dependents")

Wage information: Information about wages, taxes withheld, social security wages, social security taxes, medicare wages, medicare taxes, and state income taxes given in the problem would be reported on a W-2 form. TurboTax will prompt you for the numbers. Enter as asked. Note that Social Security wages are generally equal to Wages. They can be different if certain fringe benefits are provided, or if the wages are over the limit of $72,600 for 1999. Also, Medicare wages are normally the same as the wages. After you have entered the Medicare tax, there are no more numbers to enter on the W-2. You are asked about Boxes 13-15, but these do not apply to Mary, so skip them by clicking on "Continue." Then you are asked about state wages and withholding. State wages are the same as federal and Mary's state withholdings are 0. There are no local wages or withholdings. When you have finished entering the W-2 information, click on the "Done With W-2s" button.

Unreported tips: None

Other types of income: The only other type of income Mary has is interest income.

Interest: Mary has $680 interest income. Click as directed to indicate the interest is taxable (since it is from a savings account). Enter the payer's name and the amount. Then answer "No" to questions about other types of interest and accounts. There are no interest income adjustments necessary.

Other types of income, losses, or special accounts: None

Deductions: None

Credits: None

Other taxes (such as the Alternative Minimum Tax): Mary is not subject to any.

Note that in the upper right-hand corner of the screen, it is noted that Mary has a tax refund of $19.

Complete the interview process by clicking the appropriate buttons (e.g., No, Next, or Continue).

Now, all that is left is to save the file and print the return. To save the file, just click on File (located in the upper left-hand corner of the screen). Then, click on Save. To print, click on the "8. Print and File" button in the EasyStep Progress Bar. Then, click on "Print for Mailing." On the next screen, click on "Print Selected Returns." Click on "Done with Printing and Filing" when appropriate.

To terminate your session with TurboTax, click on the File menu item in the upper left-hand corner of the screen. Then, click on "Exit TurboTax." Click on "Yes" if you are asked to save your file.

The following pages include a completed tax return for Mary Brown. Note that the preparer line indicates that the return was "Self-prepared." Recall that this is the personal 1040 version of TurboTax and by license agreement, it may not be used by paid preparers. The Pro Series is designed for tax return preparers. For class purposes, just write your name to the right of "Self-prepared" and hand it in.

Mary Brown
345 Florida Ave.
Acme, MI 49610

1999 U. S. INDIVIDUAL INCOME TAX RETURN SUMMARY

Adjusted Gross Income	$	4,830
Taxable Income	$	530
Total Tax	$	81
Total Payments	$	100
Refund	$	19
Effective Tax Rate		15.28 %

INSTRUCTIONS FOR ELECTRONIC FILING

If you're filing electronically, please refer to the Electronic Filing Instructions on the Electronic Filing Form for detailed step by step instructions.

INSTRUCTIONS FOR MAILING YOUR RETURN

Your federal Form 1040A shows a refund of $19.
Please mail your return to the following IRS address postmarked by Monday, April 17, 2000.

    Internal Revenue Service Center
    Cincinnati, OH 45999-0015

Be sure to sign and date your return and include the proper amount of postage on the envelope.

ATTACHMENTS

Attach the first copy or Copy B of Form(s) W-2 to the front of your Form 1040A.

KEEP THIS PAGE FOR YOUR RECORDS -- DO NOT MAIL.

Form **1040A**

Department of the Treasury   Internal Revenue Service

U.S. Individual Income Tax Return (99) 1999

IRS use only   Do not write or staple in this space.

OMB No. 1545-0085

Label

(see the instructions.)

Use the IRS label.

Otherwise, please print or type.

Your First Name and Initial	Last Name	Your Social Security Number
Mary	Brown	345-23-4567
If a Joint Return, Spouse's First Name and Initial	Last Name	Spouse's Social Security Number

Home Address (number and street). If You Have a P.O. Box, See Instructions.   Apt Number

345 Florida Ave.

City, Town or Post Office, State, and ZIP Code. If You Have a Foreign Address, See Instructions.

Acme   MI   49610

Important!

You **must** enter your SSN(s) above.

Presidential Election Campaign Fund (See instructions.)

	Yes	No
Do you want 3 to go to this fund?	X	
If a joint return, does your spouse want 3 to go to this fund?		

Note: Checking 'Yes' will not change your tax or reduce your refund.

Filing status

Check only one box.

1 [X] Single

2 [ ] Married filing joint return (even if only one had income)

3 [ ] Married filing separate return. Enter spouse's social security number above and full name here ....

4 [ ] Head of household (with qualifying person). (See instructions.) If the qualifying person is a child but not your dependent, enter this child's name here .

5 [ ] Qualifying widow(er) with dependent child (year spouse died 19   ). (See instructions.)

Exemptions

6a [ ] **Yourself.** If your parent (or someone else) can claim you as a dependent on his or her tax return, **do not** check box 6a ....

b [ ] **Spouse**

No. of boxes checked on 6a and 6b .....

c **Dependents.**

If more than seven dependents, see instructions.

(1) First name Last name	(2) Dependent's social security number	(3) Dependent's relationship to you	(4) if qualifying child for child tax credit

No. of your children on 6c who:

lived with you ......

did not live with you due to divorce or separation .....

Dependents on 6c not entered above

d Total number of exemptions claimed ....

Add numbers entered on lines above ....

Income

Attach Copy B of your Form(s) W-2 here. Also attach Form(s) 1099-R if tax was withheld.

If you did not get a W-2, see instructions.

Enclose, but do not staple, any payment.

7 Wages, salaries, tips, etc. Attach Form(s) W-2	7	4,150.
8a **Taxable** interest. Attach Schedule 1 if required	8a	680.
b Tax-exempt interest. **Do not** include on line 8a 8b		
9 Ordinary dividends. Attach Schedule 1 if required	9	
10a Total IRA distributions 10a	10b Taxable amount 10b	
11a Total pensions and annuities 11a	11b Taxable amount 11b	
12 Unemployment compensation, qualified state tuition program earnings, and Alaska Permanent Fund dividends	12	
13a Social security benefits..................... 13a	13b Taxable amount 13b	
14 Add lines 7 through 13b (far right column). This is your **total income**	14	4,830.

Adjusted gross income

15 IRA deduction (see instructions)........................... 15		
16 Student loan interest deduction (see instructions) 16		
17 Add lines 15 and 16. These are your **total adjustments**	17	
18 Subtract line 17 from line 14. This is your **adjusted gross income**	18	4,830.

BAA For Paperwork Reduction Act Notice, see instructions.

Form **1040A** (1999)

Mary Brown   345-23-4567

Taxable income

19 Enter the amount from line 18 .... | **19** | 4,830.

20a Check if:
☐ **You** were 65 or older   ☐ Blind
☐ **Spouse** was 65 or older ☐ Blind — Enter number of boxes checked .. | **20a** | ☐

b If you are married filing separately and your spouse itemizes deductions, see instructions and check here .... | **20b** | ☐

21 Enter the **standard deduction** for your filing status. **But** see instructions if you checked any box on line 20a or 20b **or** if someone can claim you as a dependent.
Single 4,300   Married filing jointly or Qualifying widow(er) 7,200
Head of household 6,350   Married filing separately 3,600 .... | **21** | 4,300.

22 Subtract line 21 from line 19. If line 21 is more than line 19, enter 0 ..... | **22** | 530.

23 Multiply 2,750 by the total number of exemptions claimed on line 6d ..... | **23** | 0.

24 Subtract line 23 from line 22. If line 23 is more than line 22, enter 0. This is your **taxable income** .... | **24** | 530.

Tax, credits, and payments

25 Find the tax on the amount on line 24 (see instructions) .... | **25** | 81.

26 Credit for child and dependent care expenses. Attach Schedule 2 ...... | **26** |

27 Credit for the elderly or the disabled. Attach Schedule 3 ..... | **27** |

28 Child tax credit (see instructions) .... | **28** |

29 Education credits. Attach Form 8863 .... | **29** |

30 Adoption credit. Attach Form 8839 .... | **30** |

31 Add lines 26 through 30. These are your **total credits** .... | **31** |

32 Subtract line 31 from line 25. If line 31 is more than line 25, enter 0 ..... | **32** | 81.

33 Advance earned income credit payments from Form(s) W-2 .... | **33** |

34 Add lines 32 and 33. This is your **total tax** .... | **34** | 81.

35 Total federal income tax withheld from Forms W-2 and 1099 .... | **35** | 100.

36 1999 estimated tax payments and amount applied from 1998 return | **36** |

37a **Earned income credit.** Attach Schedule EIC if you have a qualifying child ...... | **37a** | No

b Nontaxable earned income: amount _____ and type _____

38 Additional child tax credit. Attach Form 8812 .... | **38** |

39 Add lines 35, 36, 37a and 38. These are your **total payments** ..... | **39** | 100.

Refund

Have it directly deposited! See instructions and fill in 41b, 41c, and 41d.

40 If line 39 is more than line 34, subtract line 34 from line 39. This is the amount you **overpaid** ...... | **40** | 19.

41a Amount of line 40 you want **refunded to you** .... | **41a** | 19.

b Routing number .... _____   c Type: ☐ Checking ☐ Savings
d Account number .... _____

42 Amount of line 40 you want **applied to your 2000 estimated tax** ..... | **42** |

Amount you owe

43 If line 34 is more than line 39, subtract line 39 from line 34. This is the **amount you owe**. For details on how to pay, see instructions .... | **43** |

44 Estimated tax penalty (see instructions) .... **44** |

Sign Here

Under penalties of perjury, I declare that I have examined this return and accompanying schedules and statements, and to the best of my knowledge and belief, they are true, correct, and accurately list all amounts and sources of income I received during the tax year. Declaration of preparer (other than the taxpayer) is based on all information of which the preparer has any knowledge.

Joint return? See instructions.
Keep a copy for your records.

Your Signature | Date | Your Occupation: Cashier | Daytime Telephone Number (optional)
Spouse's Signature. If Joint Return, **Both** Must Sign. | Date | Spouse's Occupation |

Paid Preparer's Use Only

Preparer's Signature | Date | Check if self-employed ☐ | Preparer's SSN or PTIN
Firm's Name (or yours if self-employed) and Address: SELF-PREPARED | EIN | ZIP Code

Schedule 1
(Form 1040A)

Department of the Treasury   Internal Revenue Service

Interest and Ordinary Dividends for Form 1040A Filers

(99)   **1999**

OMB No. 1545-0085

Name(s) Shown on Form 1040A

Mary Brown

Your Social Security Number

345-23-4567

Part I

Interest

(See instructions for Form 1040A, line 8a.)

Note: If you received a Form 1099-INT, Form 1099-OID, or substitute statement from a brokerage firm, enter the firm's name and the total interest shown on that form.

1 List name of payer. If any interest is from a seller-financed mortgage and the buyer used the property as a personal residence, see instructions and list this interest first. Also, show that buyer's social security number and address.

		Amount
Bank of Acme	1	680.00

2 Add the amounts on line 1 . . . . | 2 | 680.00

3 Excludable interest on series EE and I U.S. savings bonds issued after 1989 from Form 8815, line 14. You **must** attach Form 8815 . . . . | 3 |

4 Subtract line 3 from line 2. Enter the result here and on Form 1040A, line 8a . . . . | 4 | 680.00

Part II

Ordinary Dividends

(See instructions for Form 1040A, line 9.)

Note: If you received a Form 1099-DIV or substitute statement from a brokerage firm, enter the firm's name and the ordinary dividends shown on that form.

5 List name of payer

		Amount
	5	

6 Add the amounts on line 5. Enter the total here and on Form 1040A, line 9 . . . . | 6 |

BAA For Paperwork Reduction Act Notice, see Form 1040A instructions.

Schedule 1 (Form 1040A) 1999

PROBLEM 2 Larry and Pat Graham

Objective: Sample problem and solution. Joint return with child care, gain from sale of stock, and itemized deductions.

Larry Graham, is married to Pat Graham. Larry was born on July 10, 1951; Pat, on January 20, 1953. Larry works as a contract estimator for Madison Construction Co. Larry's W-2 reports the following information:

Address	456 Edgewood Ave., Madison WI 53706
Social security number	234-87-5643
Employer	Madison Construction Co., 432 Wisconsin
Wages	$34,000
Federal income taxes W/H	$ 3,454
State income taxes W/H	$ 2,080
Social security taxes	$ 1,108
Medicare taxes	$ 493

Pat is a stock broker with Mid-West Investors, and reports the following W-2 information:

Address	456 Edgewood Ave., Madison WI 53706
Social security number	243-12-3000
Employer	Mid-West Investors, 34 State Street, Madison,
Wages	$35,000
Federal income taxes W/H	$ 4,250
State income taxes W/H	$ 2,800
Social security taxes	$ 2,170
Medicare taxes	$ 507

The Grahams have two children: Larry, Jr. who is 5 months, and Michelle, who is 6 years old. Larry, Jr. SSN is 233-11-2311 and Michelle's social security number is 233-44-5566. Their telephone for state return purposes is 608-555-5555.

In addition to the salary income above, Larry and Pat incurred the following tax transactions:

1.   Interest income from the Bank of Wisconsin, $455; interest income from State of Wisconsin bonds, $250.

2.   Dividends were received on RayOVac Batteries stock of $345 and from Wisconsin Cheese Company of $125.

3.   The Grahams had no interest in any foreign accounts or trusts.

4.   Pat purchased 100 shares of Apple Computer stock on April 10, 1999 for $1,300. She sold the stock August 22, 1999 for $1,200.

5.   Larry purchased 500 shares of SONY Inc. on March 5, 1987 for $22,500. He sold these also on August 22, 1999, for $30,000. The Grahams executed no other stock transactions during the year.

6.   Child care for the Grahams' children was provided by Madison Care, 1299 Regent St., Madison, WI 53706, ID-Number 66-2345677. The Grahams paid $2,600 for care for both children.

7.   The Grahams received a refund of Wisconsin income taxes of $85 in June of the current tax year. On their tax return filed last year, they had total itemized deductions of $14,300, which included $3,500 of state income taxes. Taxable income on that return was $48,700.

8.   Potential itemized deductions for this year are the following:

   a.   Real estate taxes, $1,000
   b.   Personal property taxes based upon value of cars, $120
   c.   Home mortgage interest reported on Form 1098, $7,400
          (paid to Badger Credit Union)
   d.   Interest on bank credit cards, $1,050
   e.   Contributions to the University of Wisconsin, $1,500
   f.   Fee for preparation of income tax returns, $450

9.   Larry elects to support the Presidential Election Campaign Fund; Pat does not.

REQUIRED: Complete the federal income tax return.

Larry & Pat Graham
456 Edgewood Ave.
Madison, WI 53706

1999 U. S. INDIVIDUAL INCOME TAX RETURN SUMMARY

Adjusted Gross Income	$	77,410
Taxable Income	$	51,510
Total Tax	$	6,719
Total Payments	$	7,704
Refund	$	985
Effective Tax Rate		13.04 %

INSTRUCTIONS FOR ELECTRONIC FILING

If you're filing electronically, please refer to the Electronic Filing Instructions
on the Electronic Filing Form for detailed step by step instructions.

INSTRUCTIONS FOR MAILING YOUR RETURN

Your federal Form 1040 shows a refund of $985.
Please mail your return to the following IRS address postmarked by
Monday, April 17, 2000.

    Internal Revenue Service Center
    Kansas City, MO 64999-0102

Be sure to sign and date your return and include the proper amount
of postage on the envelope.

ATTACHMENTS

Attach the first copy or Copy B of Form(s) W-2 to the front of your
Form 1040.

KEEP THIS PAGE FOR YOUR RECORDS -- DO NOT MAIL.

Form **1040** Department of the Treasury   Internal Revenue Service

U.S. Individual Income Tax Return **1999** (99) IRS use only Do not write or staple in this space.

For the year Jan 1-Dec 31, 1999, or other tax year beginning ____ , 1999, ending ____ , OMB No. 1545-0074

Label (See instructions.)	Your First Name: **Larry**	MI	Last Name: **Graham**	Your Social Security Number: **234-87-5643**
Use the IRS label. Otherwise, please print or type.	If a Joint Return, Spouse's First Name: **Pat**	MI	Last Name: **Graham**	Spouse's Social Security Number: **243-12-3000**

Home Address (number and street). If You Have a P.O. Box, See Instructions. **456 Edgewood Ave.**   Apartment No.

Important! You **must** enter your social security number(s) above.

City, Town or Post Office. If You Have a Foreign Address, See Instructions. **Madison**   State **WI** ZIP Code **53706**

Presidential Election Campaign (See instructions.)

	Yes	No	Note: Checking 'Yes' will not change your tax or reduce your refund.
Do you want 3 to go to this fund?	X		
If a joint return, does your spouse want 3 to go to this fund?		X	

Filing Status

Check only one box.

1 ☐ Single
2 ☒ Married filing joint return (even if only one had income)
3 ☐ Married filing separate return. Enter spouse's SSN above & full name here ... ____
4 ☐ Head of household (with qualifying person). (See instructions.) If the qualifying person is a child but not your dependent, enter this child's name here ... ____
5 ☐ Qualifying widow(er) with dependent child (year spouse died 19 ____). (See instructions.)

Exemptions

6a ☒ **Yourself.** If your parent (or someone else) can claim you as a dependent on his or her tax return, **do not** check box 6a ....

No. of boxes checked on 6a and 6b **2**

b ☒ **Spouse** ....

c **Dependents:**

(1) First name Last name	(2) Dependent's social security number	(3) Dependent's relationship to you	(4) if qualifying child for child tax credit (see instructions)
Larry Graham Jr.	233-11-2311	Son	X
Michelle Graham	233-44-5566	Daughter	X

No. of your children on 6c who:
lived with you **2**
did not live with you due to divorce or separation (see instructions) .. ____

If more than six dependents, see instructions.

Dependents on 6c not entered above .... ____

d Total number of exemptions claimed .... Add numbers entered on lines above . **4**

Income

Attach Copy B of your Forms W-2 and W-2G here. Also attach Form(s) 1099-R if tax was withheld.

If you did not get a W-2, see instructions.

7 Wages, salaries, tips, etc. Attach Form(s) W-2	7	69,000.
8a **Taxable** interest. Attach Schedule B if required	8a	455.
b **Tax-exempt** interest. **Do not** include on line 8a .... 8b 250.		
9 Ordinary dividends. Attach Schedule B if required	9	470.
10 Taxable refunds, credits, or offsets of state and local income taxes (see instructions)	10	85.
11 Alimony received	11	
12 Business income or (loss). Attach Schedule C or C-EZ...........................	12	
13 Capital gain or (loss). Attach Schedule D if required. If not required, check here .... ☐	13	7,400.
14 Other gains or (losses). Attach Form 4797	14	
15a Total IRA distributions ..... 15a b Taxable amount (see instrs) ..	15b	
16a Total pensions & annuities . 16a b Taxable amount (see instrs) ..	16b	
17 Rental real estate, royalties, partnerships, S corporations, trusts, etc. Attach Schedule E ..	17	
18 Farm income or (loss). Attach Schedule F	18	
19 Unemployment compensation	19	
20a Social security benefits ..... 20a b Taxable amount (see instrs) ..	20b	
21 Other income. List type & amount (see instrs) _____	21	
22 Add the amounts in the far right column for lines 7 through 21. This is your **total income**	22	77,410.

Enclose, but do not staple, any payment. Also, please use **Form 1040-V.**

Adjusted Gross Income

23 IRA deduction (see instructions)...........................	23		
24 Student loan interest deduction (see instructions)	24		
25 Medical savings account deduction. Attach Form 8853	25		
26 Moving expenses. Attach Form 3903	26		
27 One-half of self-employment tax. Attach Schedule SE	27		
28 Self-employed health insurance deduction (see instructions) .	28		
29 Keogh and self-employed SEP and SIMPLE plans	29		
30 Penalty on early withdrawal of savings	30		
31a Alimony paid b Recipient's SSN .... _____	31a		
32 Add lines 23 through 31a		32	
33 Subtract line 32 from line 22. This is your **adjusted gross income**		33	77,410.

BAA For Disclosure, Privacy Act, and Paperwork Reduction Act Notice, see instructions.   Form **1040** (1999)

FDIA0112 11/16/99

Tax and Credits

34	Amount from line 33 (adjusted gross income)	34	77,410.

35a Check if: ☐ **You** were 65/older, ☐ Blind; ☐ **Spouse** was 65/older, ☐ Blind.
Add the number of boxes checked above and enter the total here .... **35a** ☐

b If you are married filing separately and your spouse itemizes deductions or you were a dual-status alien, see instructions and check here .... **35b** ☐

Standard Deduction for Most People

36 Enter your **itemized deductions** from Schedule A, line 28, **Or standard deduction** shown on the left. **But** see instructions to find your standard deduction if you checked any box on line 35a or 35b **or** if someone can claim you as a dependent ....

36	14,900.
37	Subtract line 36 from line 34	62,510.

38 If line 34 is $94,975 or less, multiply $2,750 by the total number of exemptions claimed on line 6d. If line 34 is over $94,975, see the worksheet in the instructions for the amount to enter .... **38** 11,000.

39 **Taxable income.** Subtract line 38 from line 37. If line 38 is more than line 37, enter -0- .... **39** 51,510.

40 **Tax** (see instrs). Check if any tax is from **a** ☐ Form(s) 8814 **b** ☐ Form 4972 .... **40** 8,239.

Single: 4,300

Head of household: 6,350

Married filing jointly or Qualifying widow(er): 7,200

Married filing separately: 3,600

41	Credit for child and dependent care expenses. Attach Form 2441	41	520.
42	Credit for the elderly or the disabled. Attach Schedule R	42	
43	Child tax credit (see instructions)	43	1,000.
44	Education credits. Attach Form 8863	44	
45	Adoption credit. Attach Form 8839	45	
46	Foreign tax credit. Attach Form 1116 if required	46	
47	Other. Check if from .. **a** ☐ Form 3800 **b** ☐ Form 8396 **c** ☐ Form 8801 **d** ☐ Form (specify) _____	47	

48	Add lines 41 through 47. These are your **total credits**	48	1,520.
49	Subtract line 48 from line 40. If line 48 is more than line 40, enter -0-	49	6,719.

Other Taxes

50	Self-employment tax. Attach Schedule SE	50	
51	Alternative minimum tax. Attach Form 6251	51	
52	Social security and Medicare tax on tip income not reported to employer. Attach Form 4137	52	
53	Tax on IRAs, other retirement plans, and MSAs. Attach Form 5329 if required	53	
54	Advance earned income credit payments from Form(s) W-2	54	
55	Household employment taxes. Attach Schedule H	55	
56	Add lines 49-55. This is your **total tax**	56	6,719.

Payments

57	Federal income tax withheld from Forms W-2 and 1099	57	7,704.
58	1999 estimated tax payments and amount applied from 1998 return	58	

59a Earned income credit. Attach Schedule EIC if you have a qualifying child.

b Nontaxable earned income: amount _____ and type _____ **59a**

60	Additional child tax credit. Attach Form 8812	60
61	Amount paid with request for extension to file (see instructions)	61
62	Excess social security and RRTA tax withheld (see instrs) ...	62
63	Other payments. Check if from ..... **a** ☐ Form 2439 **b** ☐ Form 4136	63

64	Add lines 57, 58, 59a, and 60 through 63. These are your **total payments**	64	7,704.

Refund

Have it directly deposited! See instructions and fill in 66b, 66c, and 66d.

65	If line 64 is more than line 56, subtract line 56 from line 64. This is the amount you **Overpaid**	65	985.
66a	Amount of line 65 you want **Refunded to You**	66a	985.

b Routing number .... _____ **c** Type: ☐ Checking ☐ Savings
d Account number .... _____

67	Amount of line 65 you want **Applied to Your 2000 Estimated Tax**	67	

Amount You Owe

68	If line 56 is more than line 64, subtract line 64 from line 56. This is the **Amount You Owe.** For details on how to pay, see instructions	68
69	Estimated tax penalty. Also include on line 68	69	

Sign Here

Joint return? See instructions.

Keep a copy for your records.

Under penalties of perjury, I declare that I have examined this return and accompanying schedules and statements, and to the best of my knowledge and belief, they are true, correct, and complete. Declaration of preparer (other than taxpayer) is based on all information of which preparer has any knowledge.

Your Signature	Date	Your Occupation Estimator	Daytime Telephone Number (optional)
Spouse's Signature. If a Joint Return, **Both** Must Sign.	Date	Spouse's Occupation Stock Broker	

Paid Preparer's Use Only

Preparer's Signature	Date	Check if self-employed ☐	Preparer's SSN or PTIN
Firm's Name (or yours if self-employed) and Address	Self-prepared	EIN	ZIP Code

Schedule A
(Form 1040)

Department of the Treasury
Internal Revenue Service   (99)

Itemized Deductions

Attach to Form 1040.
See Instructions for Schedule A (Form 1040).

OMB No. 1545-0074

1999
07

Name(s) Shown on Form 1040

Larry & Pat Graham

Your Social Security Number

234-87-5643

Medical and Dental Expenses		**Caution:** Do not include expenses reimbursed or paid by others.			
	1	Medical and dental expenses (see instructions)	1		
	2	Enter amount from Form 1040, line 34 ..... | 2 |			
	3	Multiply line 2 above by 7.5% (.075)	3		
	4	Subtract line 3 from line 1. If line 3 is more than line 1, enter -0-		4	
Taxes You Paid (See instructions.)	5	State and local income taxes	5	4,880.	
	6	Real estate taxes (see instructions)	6	1,000.	
	7	Personal property taxes	7	120.	
	8	Other taxes. List type and amount	8		
	9	Add lines 5 through 8		9	6,000.
Interest You Paid (See instructions.)	10	Home mortgage interest and points reported to you on Form 1098	10	7,400.	
	11	Home mortgage interest not reported to you on Form 1098. If paid to the person from whom you bought the home, see instructions and show that person's name, identifying number, and address	11		
Note: Personal interest is not deductible.	12	Points not reported to you on Form 1098. See instructions for special rules	12		
	13	Investment interest. Attach Form 4952 if required. (See instructions.)	13		
	14	Add lines 10 through 13		14	7,400.
Gifts to Charity If you made a gift and got a benefit for it, see instructions.	15	Gifts by cash or check. If you made any gift of 250 or more, see instructions	15	1,500.	
	16	Other than by cash or check. If any gift of 250 or more, see instructions. You **Must** attach Form 8283 if over 500	16		
	17	Carryover from prior year	17		
	18	Add lines 15 through 17		18	1,500.
Casualty and Theft Losses	19	Casualty or theft loss(es). Attach Form 4684. (See instructions.)		19	
Job Expenses and Most Other Miscellaneous Deductions (See instructions for expenses to deduct here.)	20	Unreimbursed employee expenses job travel, union dues, job education, etc. You **Must** attach Form 2106 or 2106-EZ if required. (See instructions.)	20		
	21	Tax preparation fees	21	450.	
	22	Other expenses investment, safe deposit box, etc. List type and amount	22		
	23	Add lines 20 through 22	23	450.	
	24	Enter amount from Form 1040, line 34 ..... | 24 | 77,410.			
	25	Multiply line 24 above by 2% (.02)	25	1,548.	
	26	Subtract line 25 from line 23. If line 25 is more than line 23, enter -0-		26	0.
Other Miscellaneous Deductions	27	Other from list in the instructions. List type and amount		27	
Total Itemized Deductions	28	Is Form 1040, line 34, over 126,600 (over 63,300 if married filing separately)?			
		[X] **No.** Your deduction is not limited. Add the amounts in the far right column for lines 4 through 27. Also, enter this amount on Form 1040, line 36.		28	14,900.
		[ ] **Yes.** Your deduction may be limited. See instructions for the amount to enter.			

BAA For Paperwork Reduction Act Notice, see separate instructions.

Schedule A (Form 1040) 1999

FDIA0301   10/27/99

Name(s) Shown on Form 1040. Do Not Enter Name and Social Security Number if Shown on Schedule A. | **Your Social Security Number**

Larry & Pat Graham

234-87-5643

Schedule B   Interest and Ordinary Dividends
08

Note: If you had over 400 in taxable interest income, you must also complete Part III.

			Amount
Part I **Interest**	**1**	List name of payer. If any interest is from a seller-financed mortgage and the buyer used the property as a personal residence, see the instructions and list this interest first. Also, show that buyer's social security number and address	
		Bank of Wisconsin	455.00
(See instructions for Form 1040, line 8a.)		State of Wisconsin	250.00
Note: If you received a Form 1099-INT, Form 1099-OID, or substitute statement from a brokerage firm, list the firm's name as the payer and enter the total interest shown on that form.		**1**	
		Subtotal	705.00
		Tax-Exempt Interest	-250.00
	2	Add the amounts on line 1 .... **2**	455.00
	3	Excludable interest on series EE and I U.S. savings bonds issued after 1989 from Form 8815, line 14. You **Must** attach Form 8815 .... **3**	
	4	Subtract line 3 from line 2. Enter the result here and on Form 1040, line 8a **4**	455.00

Note: If you had over 400 in ordinary dividends, you must also complete Part III.

			Amount
Part II **Ordinary Dividends**	**5**	List name of payer. Include only ordinary dividends. If you received any capital gain distributions, see the instructions for Form 1040, line 13	
		RayOVac Batteries	345.00
(See instructions for Form 1040, line 8a.)		Wisconsin Cheese Company	125.00
Note: If you received a Form 1099-DIV, or substitute statement from a brokerage firm, list the firm's name as the payer and enter the ordinary dividends shown on that form.		**5**	
	6	Add the amounts on line 5. Enter the total here and on Form 1040, line 9 .... **6**	470.00

			Yes	No
Part III **Foreign Accounts and Trusts** (See instructions.)	You must complete this part if you **(a)** had over 400 of interest or ordinary dividends; **(b)** had a foreign account; or **(c)** received a distribution from, or were a grantor of, or a transferor to, a foreign trust.			
	7a At any time during 1999, did you have an interest in or a signature or other authority over a financial account in a foreign country, such as a bank account, securities account, or other financial account? See instructions for exceptions and filing requirements for Form TD F 90-22.1			X
	b If 'yes,' enter the name of the foreign country...			
	8 During 1999, did you receive a distribution from, or were you the grantor of, or transferor to, a foreign trust? If 'yes,' you may have to file Form 3520. See instructions			X

BAA For Paperwork Reduction Act Notice, see Form 1040 instructions.   FDIA0401 10/13/99   Schedule **B** (Form 1040) 1999

Schedule D
(Form 1040)

Department of the Treasury
Internal Revenue Service (99)

Capital Gains and Losses

Attach to Form 1040.   See instructions for Schedule D (Form 1040).
Use Schedule D-1 for more space to list transactions for lines 1 and 8.

OMB No. 1545-0074

1999

12

Name(s) Shown on Form 1040

Larry & Pat Graham

Your Social Security Number

234-87-5643

Part I   Short-Term Capital Gains and Losses   Assets Held One Year or Less

(a) Description of property (Example: 100 shares XYZ Co)	(b) Date acquired (Mo, day, yr)	(c) Date sold (Mo, day, yr)	(d) Sales price (see instructions)	(e) Cost or other basis (see instructions)	(f) Gain or (Loss) Subtract (e) from (d)	
1 100 Shares Apple Computer	04/10/99	08/22/99	1,200.00	1,300.00	-100.00	

2 Enter your short-term totals, if any, from Schedule D-1, line 2	2			
3 **Total short-term sales price amounts.** Add column (d) of lines 1 and 2	3	1,200.00		
4 Short-term gain from Form 6252 and short-term gain or (loss) from Forms 4684, 6781, and 8824	4			
5 Net short-term gain or (loss) from partnerships, S corporations, estates, and trusts from Schedule(s) K-1	5			
6 Short-term capital loss carryover. Enter the amount, if any, from line 8 of your 1998 Capital Loss Carryover Worksheet	6			
7 **Net short-term capital gain or (loss).** Combine lines 1 through 6 in column (f)	7			-100.

Part II   Long-Term Capital Gains and Losses   Assets Held More Than One Year

(a) Description of property (Example: 100 shares XYZ Co)	(b) Date acquired (Mo, day, yr)	(c) Date sold (Mo, day, yr)	(d) Sales price (see instructions)	(e) Cost or other basis (see instructions)	(f) Gain or (Loss) Subtract (e) from (d)	(g) 28% Rate Gain or (Loss) * (see instructions below)
8 500 Shares Sony Inc.	03/05/87	08/22/99	30,000.00	22,500.00	7,500.00	

9 Enter your long-term totals, if any, from Schedule D-1, line 9	9			
10 **Total long-term sales price amounts.** Add column (d) of lines 8 and 9	10	30,000.00		
11 Gain from Form 4797, Part I; long-term gain from Forms 2439 and 6252; and long-term gain or (loss) from Forms 4684, 6781, and 8824	11			
12 Net long-term gain or (loss) from partnerships, S corporations, estates, and trusts from Schedule(s) K-1	12			
13 Capital gain distributions. See instructions	13			
14 Long-term capital loss carryover. Enter in both columns (f) and (g) the amount, if any, from line 13 of your 1998 Capital Loss Carryover Worksheet	14			
15 Combine lines 8 through 14 in column (g)	15			
16 **Net long-term capital gain or (loss).** Combine lines 8 through 14 in column (f)	16	7,500.		

Next: Go to Part III on page 2.

* **28% Rate Gain or Loss** includes **all** 'collectibles gains and losses' (as defined in the instructions) and up to 50% of the eligible gain on qualified small business stock (see instructions).

BAA **For Paperwork Reduction Act Notice, see Form 1040 instructions.**

Schedule **D** (Form 1040) 1999

FDIA0612   10/13/99

Part III   Summary of Parts I and II

17	Combine lines 7 and 16. If a loss, go to line 18. If a gain, enter the gain on Form 1040, line 13 .... **17**	7,400.

Next: Complete Form 1040 through line 39. Then, go to **Part IV** to figure your tax if:

Both lines 16 and 17 are gains, **and**

Form 1040, line 39, is more than zero.

18 If line 17 is a loss, enter here and as a (loss) on Form 1040, line 13, the **smaller** of these losses:

The loss on line 17, **or**

(3,000) or, if married filing separately, (1,500) **18**

Next: Skip **Part IV** below. Instead, complete Form 1040 through line 37. Then, complete the **Capital Loss Carryover Worksheet** in the instructions if:

The loss on line 17 exceeds the loss on line 18, **or**

Form 1040, line 37, is a loss.

Part IV   Tax Computation Using Maximum Capital Gains Rates

19	Enter your taxable income from Form 1040, line 39...............................	**19**		51,510.
20	Enter the **smaller** of line 16 or line 17 of Schedule D	**20**	7,400.	
21	If you are filing Form 4952, enter the amount from Form 4952, line 4e	**21**		
22	Subtract line 21 from line 20. If zero or less, enter -0-	**22**	7,400.	
23	Combine lines 7 and 15. If zero or less, enter -0-	**23**	0.	
24	Enter the **smaller** of line 15 or line 23, but not less than zero	**24**	0.	
25	Enter your unrecaptured section 1250 gain, if any, from line 16 of the worksheet in the instructions	**25**		
26	Add lines 24 and 25	**26**	0.	
27	Subtract line 26 from line 22. If zero or less, enter -0-	**27**		7,400.
28	Subtract line 27 from line 19. If zero or less, enter -0-	**28**		44,110.
29	Enter the **smaller** of: The amount on line 19, **or** 25,750 if single; 43,050 if married filing jointly or qualifying widow(er); 21,525 if married filing separately; or 34,550 if head of household	**29**		43,050.
30	Enter the **smaller** of line 28 or line 29	**30**	43,050.	
31	Subtract line 22 from line 19. If zero or less, enter -0-	**31**	44,110.	
32	Enter the **larger** of line 30 or line 31	**32**	44,110.	
33	Figure the tax on the amount on line 32. Use the Tax Table or Tax Rate Schedules, whichever applies	**33**		6,759.

Note: If line 29 is less than line 28, go to line 38.

34	Enter the amount from line 29	**34**		
35	Enter the amount from line 28	**35**		
36	Subtract line 35 from line 34. If zero or less, enter -0-	**36**		
37	Multiply line 36 by 10% (.10)	**37**		

Note: If line 27 is more than zero **and** equal to line 36, go to line 52.

38	Enter the **smaller** of line 19 or line 27	**38**	7,400.	
39	Enter the amount from line 36	**39**		
40	Subtract line 39 from line 38...........	**40**	7,400.	
41	Multiply line 40 by 20% (.20)	**41**		1,480.

Note: If line 25 is zero or blank, skip lines 42 through 47 and read the note above line 48.

42	Enter the **smaller** of line 22 or line 25	**42**		
43	Add lines 22 and 32........... **43**			
44	Enter the amount from line 19........... **44**			
45	Subtract line 44 from line 43. If zero or less, enter -0-	**45**		
46	Subtract line 45 from line 42. If zero or less, enter -0-	**46**		
47	Multiply line 46 by 25% (.25)	**47**		

Note: If line 24 is zero or blank, go to line 52.

48	Enter the amount from line 19	**48**		
49	Add lines 32, 36, 40, and 46	**49**		
50	Subtract line 49 from line 48	**50**		
51	Multiply line 50 by 28% (.28)	**51**		
52	Add lines 33, 37, 41, 47, and 51	**52**		8,239.
53	Figure the tax on the amount on line 19. Use the Tax Table or Tax Rate Schedules, whichever applies	**53**		8,831.
54	**Tax on all taxable income (including capital gains).** Enter the **smaller** of line 52 or line 53 here and on Form 1040, line 40	**54**		8,239.

Child and Dependent Care Expenses

Attach to Form 1040.
See separate instructions.

OMB No. 1545-0068

1999

21

Name(s) Shown on Form 1040	Your Social Security Number
Larry & Pat Graham	234-87-5643

Before you begin, you need to understand the following terms. See **Definitions** in the instructions.

Dependent Care Benefits	Qualifying Person(s)	Qualified Expenses	Earned Income

Part I   **Persons or Organizations Who Provided the Care**   You **must** complete this part.
(If you need more space, use the bottom of page 2.)

1	(a) Care provider's name	(b) Address (no., street, apt no., city, state, and ZIP code)	(c) Identifying number (SSN or EIN)	(d) Amount paid (see instructions)
	Madison Care	1299 Regent St. Madison, WI 53706	66-2345677	2,600.00

Did you receive **dependent care benefits?**	**No**	Complete only Part II below.
	Yes	Complete Part III on page 2 next.

Caution: *If the care was provided in your home, you may owe employment taxes. See the instructions for Form 1040, line 55.*

Part II   **Credit for Child and Dependent Care Expenses**

2   Information about your **qualifying person(s).** If you have more than two qualifying persons, see the instructions.

(a) Qualifying person's name		(b) Qualifying person's social security number	(c) Qualified expenses you incurred and paid in 1999 for the person listed in column (a)
First	Last		
Larry	Graham Jr.	233-11-2311	1,300.
Michelle	Graham	233-44-5566	1,300.

3	Add the amounts in column (c) of line 2. **Do not** enter more than 2,400 for one qualifying person or 4,800 for two or more persons. If you completed Part III, enter the amount from line 24	**3**		2,600.
4	Enter **your earned income**	**4**		34,000.
5	If married filing a joint return, enter **your spouse's** earned income (if your spouse was a student or was disabled, see the instructions); **all others,** enter the amount from line 4	**5**		35,000.
6	Enter the **smallest** of line 3, 4, or 5	**6**		2,600.
7	Enter the amount from Form 1040, line 34	**7**	77,410.	

8   Enter on line 8 the decimal amount shown below that applies to the amount on line 7

If line 7 is				If line 7 is					
Over	But not over	Decimal amount is		Over	But not over	Decimal amount is			
0	10,000	.30		20,000	22,000	.24			
10,000	12,000	.29		22,000	24,000	.23			
12,000	14,000	.28		24,000	26,000	.22	**8** X		0.20
14,000	16,000	.27		26,000	28,000	.21			
16,000	18,000	.26		28,000	No limit	.20			
18,000	20,000	.25							

9	Multiply **line 6** by the decimal amount on line 8. Enter the result here and on Form 1040, line 41. But if this amount is more than the amount on Form 1040, line 40, **or** you paid 1998 expenses in 1999, see the instructions for the amount to enter on line 41	**9**		520.

BAA For Paperwork Reduction Act Notice, see separate instructions.   Form **2441** (1999)

PROBLEM 3 Carl and Christie Clennick

Objective: Self-employed taxpayer with depreciation and Section 179 deduction.

Carl and Christie Clennick, both age 36, are married and live at 1080 Schelter Road, Lincolnshire, IL 60197.   Carl, Social Security number 287-65-4321, is a self-employed carpenter. Christie is a teacher at Lincolnshire High School.   She reports the following W-2 information:

Home Address	1080 Schelter Road, Lincolnshire, IL 60197
Telephone number	217-555-5555
Social security number	345-67-8910
Employer	Lincolnshire School District, 23 Court House Road, Lincolnshire, ILL 60191, employer number 33-8765432
Wages	$ 23,000
Federal income taxes W/H	3,600
State income taxes W/H	1,080
Social security taxes	1,426
Medicare taxes	333

The Clennicks have two dependent sons - Cleveland (age 8) and Mayo (age 5).   The children's Social Security numbers are 123-45-6789 and 234-56-7890, respectively.   The Clennicks have presented you with the following tax information for the current year.

1.   The Clennicks both support the President Election Campaign Fund.

2.   The Clennicks received interest of $550 from First National Bank of Lincolnshire. They also received dividends of $525 from General Products Corporation and $125 from Acme Supplies, Inc. The Clennicks do not have an interest in any foreign accounts.

3.   For the last two years, Carl was employed as a carpenter by Lincolnshire Contractors, Inc. On January 3 of the current tax year, he started his own business - Clennick Carpenter Service, 2125 Main Street, Lincolnshire, IL, 60197, employer identification number 22-1234567. He uses the cash method of reporting.

        Carl continued to use the tools and equipment (all fully depreciated) he owned and used while employed by Lincolnshire Contractors. In addition, he purchased a new light-duty pick-up truck for $16,000 on January 5. He drove the truck 20,000 miles during the year (8,000 for personal use and 12,000 for business). He did not use the truck for any other purposes, and no one else used it. He elected to compute the cost recovery allowance for the truck using prescribed statutory percentages and he chose not to expense the truck under Section 179. Also, Carl purchased some new tools on February 1 that cost

$1,200. Carl wants to expense these tools under section 179. Carl's other income and expense items relating to his business are summarized below:

Total income	$	56,000
Expenses:		
Advertising		1,600
Bank service charges		1,100
Truck operating expenses		2,500
Insurance		1,200
Legal and professional services		1,400
Supplies		1,900
Utilities and telephone		1,300

4.   Christie attended a three-day teacher's convention in New York and incurred $600 of unreimbursed expenses for airfare and lodging.

5.   Carl and Christie each made a contribution of $2,000 to separate Individual Retirement Accounts (i.e. a total contribution of $4,000 for the two of them.) In addition Christie's employer contributed $2,400 to the Illinois State Retirement Fund on her behalf. The state retirement fund is a qualified retirement plan.

6.   The Clennicks incurred the following expenses during the current year:

a.	Estimated payments on state income tax	$740
	(Paid quarterly; last payment December 31, 1999)	
b.	Additional payment of 1998 state income tax	420
	(Paid April, 1999)	
c.	Real estate taxes on personal residence	650
d.	Home mortgage interest	980
e.	Credit card interest	300
f.	Charitable contributions (cash) to State U	800
g.	Professional dues (Christie)	940

7.   The Clennicks paid an unrelated child care service, Child Care Company, 23 Main Street, Douglas, IL 60001, $350 per month during the year. The services were provided in the Clennick's home. Child Care's EIN is 66-7788990.

8.   The Clennicks made total estimated Federal tax payments of $9,200, consisting of four $2,300 payments that were made on April 15, June 15 and September 15, 1999 and January 15, 2000.

REQUIRED: Use TurboTax to prepare and print the Federal income tax return.

PROBLEM 4 Lynn and Heather O'Keefe

Objective: Upper income taxpayer, entertainment expenses, distribution from an IRA, dependent elderly parent, and home business tax problems.

Lynn O'Keefe, age 53, is president of O'Keefes Furniture Store. He reports the following W-2 information:

Home Address	46 Germantown Rd., Chattanooga, TN 37411
Telephone	615-555-5555
Social security number	524-67-2343
Employer	O'Keefes Furniture store, 1201 Hamilton Ave., Chattanooga, TN 37401, employer number 64-1453236.
Wages	$98,000
Federal income taxes W/H	$24,640
Social security taxes	$ 3,887
Medicare taxes	$ 1,421

Heather O'Keefe, age 50, social security number 446-18-3904, works at home as a housewife.

Both Lynn and Heather want $3 of their taxes to go the to Presidential Election Campaign Fund. The O'Keefe children are grown. However, Heather's mother, Molly Shoulders, lives with them. Molly received social security of $5,400, and interest income of $5,000 during the year. She has no other income.

In addition to the income above, Lynn and Heather incurred the following tax transactions during the year:

1.   Interest income from the Hamilton National Bank, $680.

2.   Lynn received a pre-mature distribution from an IRA account of $28,500, which he used to purchase a new car.

3.   The O'Keefes have no interest in any foreign accounts or trusts.

4.   Lynn purchased 10,000 shares of Bassett Inc. stock on April 22, 1981 for $120,000. He sold the stock on August 12, 1999 for $91,200.

5.   To promote the family business, Lynn and Heather give a large party at Christmas time for all their best customers. The party cost $2,300.

6.   During the year, Lynn drove his personal automobile 30,000 miles including 3,000 miles to and from work, and 2,000 round and about town. The other 25,000 miles were related to business trips (to buy furniture). The company reimbursed him at a rate of 20 cents per mile ($5,000) for those business trips.

In addition, Lynn spent $2,500 for meals and $4,800 for lodging while on the business trips. The cost of meals was not reimbursed by his company because he forgot to file for reimbursement. If he had filed a reimbursement request, the company would have paid for the meals. The lodging was fully reimbursed by the company.

7. Heather has a good reputation as a home decorator. She writes articles and gives seminars around Chattanooga. The amount of business has been small, so she has not applied for a business license. However, she did receive the following for some of her work.

   a. Article in *Southern Living*, $250.
   b. Seminar on Medical Office decor for Erlanger Hospital, $75.
   c. "Gift" for decorating Dr. Barber's office, $100.
   d. "Gift" for doing flower arrangements at a friend's wedding, $20.
   e. McCallie Schools, for seminar on keeping rooms clean, $65.

   Note: An Itemize statement may be required to report all of these miscellaneous income items.

   To allow her to prepare outlines and hand out materials for these seminars and to write her articles, Heather spent $2,200 to purchase a personal computer and $1,500 to purchase a nice laser printer. The PC and printer were used 80% of the time to further her career as a home decorator. The balance, 20%, was used for personal letters and using Quicken to keep her check book accurate.

8. Potential itemized deductions included the following:
   a. Medical expenses included health insurance of $2,500; medical expenses paid for Molly in excess of Medicare, $12,000; Heather's eyeglasses $500.
   b. Real estate taxes, $1,000.
   c. Sales taxes on purchases, $1,520.
   d. Home mortgage interest paid to bank, $4,400.
   e. Interest on bank credit cards, $1,050.
   f. Cash contributions to their church, $5,500.
   g. Fee for preparation of personal income tax return, $600.

REQUIRED: Complete the federal income tax return.

PROBLEM 5 Crystal Ball

Objective: Single professional with IRA, investment income, moving expense and gross income problems.

Crystal Ball, age 36, is single and has no dependents. She is employed by Banker Corporation as an account manager. She reports the following W-2 information:

Home Address	2323 Westview Street, Chicago, IL 60680.
Social security number	366-55-2222
Employer	Banker Corporation, 45 Michigan Ave., Chicago, IL 60611,
	employer number 35-9765432
Wages	$63,000
Federal income taxes W/H	$15,000
State income taxes W/H	$ 2,500
Social security taxes	$ 3,887
Medicare taxes	$ 899

From Crystal's prior year tax return, you note that a federal tax refund of $325 was to be applied to current year federal taxes. You further note that she used the standard deduction for both federal and state returns last year. Lastly, you note that she received a state income tax refund of $24 during the current tax year (1999) from her prior year state return (1998). Also, you absolutely lastly note that Crystal does not have a telephone -- she hates to get calls at home.

Crystal earned interest of $1,850 from Second National Bank of Chicago. Crystal, as a new employee at Banker Corporation, is not eligible for any qualified pension plan. Accordingly, she contributed $2,000 to a new 1999 Individual Retirement Account in February, 2000. In addition, on March 7, 1999, she purchased 100 shares of Banker Corporation at a price of $86 per share. In December, 1999, she received a stock dividend of 5 shares, when the stock was valued at $90 per share. Before Crystal decided to purchase the stock she bought the Sure-fired Stock Advisor, an annual publication advising on stock trends, for $29.95.

Prior to working at Banker Corporation, Crystal worked for First Wisconsin in Milwaukee. As a part of her job offer, on January 8 of the current tax year, Banker paid Crystal $3,000 as a moving allowance.   Crystal rented a truck and move herself (a distance of 120 miles,) incurring a cost of $800 for the truck rental.   On January 4, 5, and 6, Crystal traveled to Chicago to look for an apartment. She stayed with friends from college. She took her friends out as payment for allowing her to stay with them. The cost of dinner *et al* was $340. She drove her own car, traveling a total of 300 miles. When Crystal mentioned these costs to her new boss, she was told that part of her moving allowance was to cover these kinds of costs -- she did not receive any more from Banker Corporation.

On January 31, 1999 Crystal received a check for $200 from Brewer Apartments in Milwaukee, in refund of her apartment deposit. In January of 1999, Crystal paid an apartment deposit to the Cubs Apartments in Chicago in the amount of $100. While deciding what to do with the refund check, Crystal noted that the distance from her old apartment in Milwaukee to her old job was 10 miles. Coincidentally, the distance from her new apartment to her new job is also 10 miles. Thus, she moved 120 miles and she is still 10 miles from work. But a lot closer to the Cubs games.

In April of the current tax year, Crystal was surprised by a visit from her old roommate from college, Sue. Even more astonishing to Crystal, Sue paid her $500, the amount plus some interest, she had loaned Sue in College. Sue determined that $50 of that amount was for interest. Crystal considered the entire amount to be repayment of a $450 loan that she had deducted five years earlier as a nonbusiness loan.

In September of the current tax year, Crystal was asked by a friend, Jon, to do some research/consulting work to advise him on the feasibility of a new business. Crystal spent three weekends in the Chicago library gathering information. She incurred $125 in photocopying bills. She also incurred $50 purchasing paper and other supplies that were consumed in the project. Jon agreed to pay her $400 for the project. After a total of 50 hours of work, Crystal delivered the report. Jon told her to forget it; he had decided to marry Gail and live on her money instead. In December, Jon sent Crystal a box of cheeses that cost him (or Gail) $50, with a note that said "Thanks for all your help." Jon sent these to all of his old friends.

Crystal elects to designate $3 of her taxes to the Presidential Election Campaign Fund. If Crystal is entitled to a refund, she would like to have it applied to her next year's Federal income tax as she did last year.

REQUIRED: Prepare Crystal's tax return.

PROBLEM 6 Vern Wilson

Objective: Wage earner return with miscellaneous income.

Vern Wilson has asked you to file his Federal income tax return. He is single, has no dependents, and is employed as an electrical engineer. He has given you the following information taken from his W-2 and other sources.

Home Address	221 Main Street, Newburyport, MA 01950.
Telephone	617-555-5555
Social security number	285-33-1543
Employer	Acme Components, Inc., 8 Henry Cove, Hedgemouth, MA 01999, employer number 44-5665432
Wages	$60,000
Federal income taxes W/H	$14,500
State income taxes W/H	$ 3,200
Social security taxes	$ 3,720
Medicare taxes	$ 870

1. He received interest of $1,200 on a savings account at Second National Bank, and received dividends of $800 on Acme Components, Inc. stock he owns. He has no interest in any other bank or trust accounts.

2. Vern won a $1,000 lottery prize in November.

3. Vern made a $2,000 contribution to his Individual Retirement Account (IRA) in December. Vern did not contribute to any other qualified plan, neither did his employer.

4. Vern received a refund of state income taxes in the amount of $245. In 1998, Vern took the standard deduction.

5. Acme Components greatly values Vern's work and tries to keep him happy at work. His boss redecorated his office spending $3,000 on furniture that Vern selected. Acme purchased a new personal computer with CD ROM drives and a sound card, costing $4,000 for Vern's use at home. Vern reports that 40 percent of its use was related to his job at Acme; the balance was personal use. Vern also was able to use the corporation's ocean front condo for three weeks during June. The fair market rental value of the condo is $1,000 per week. Vern was the only employee allowed to use the condo. The condo was used the rest of the year by customers only. The marginal cost to the corporation (utilities and cleaning) of Jon's using the condo was $150 per week. None of these amounts were included on Vern's W-2; the bookkeeper considered these items to be non-taxable.

6.   Vern collects things. During the year, Vern sold some of the things that he had collected for a total of $7,500. In addition, Vern purchased several new things that cost a total of $10,000. Vern also incurred transportation costs of $1,200 going to sales where he bought some things and sold some things. Vern does not keep any kind of inventory records. He estimates that the things he has in inventory cost about $30,000 but have a fair market value of $60,000. Vern does not have a business license, nor is his home in an area that is zoned for business. Vern stores all of his things at his home.

Vern's barber told him that he had to file a Schedule C and pay self-employment taxes because he was in the business of buying and selling things. Vern considers himself to have a hobby, albeit one that allows him to make some money. Ah, the joys of taxes.

7.   Vern elects to support the Presidential Election Campaign Fund.

REQUIRED: Prepare and print Vern Wilson's federal income tax return.

PROBLEM 7 George and Martha Jefferson

Objective: Kiddy tax, property transactions, itemized deductions, scholarships

George Jefferson, age 44, attends a nearby university on a full-time basis studying accounting. His Social Security number is 387-65-4346. His wife, Martha, age 45, is currently employed full time at the local First National Bank as a branch manager. The Jeffersons have two dependent daughters, Sarah (age 14) and Emily (age 12) whose Social Security numbers are 387-65-4347 and 387-65-4348, respectively.   They provide you with the following information about Martha's wages.

Home Address	123 Mountainview Lane, Monticello, Virginia 22901
Telephone	804-555-5555
Social security number	387-65-4345
Employer	First National Bank, 18 Main St., Charlottesville, VA 22916, employer number 66-5566443
Wages	$33,000
Federal income taxes W/H	$ 1,300
State income taxes W/H	$ 1,650
Social security taxes	$ 2,046
Medicare taxes	$ 478

In addition to Martha's W-2 information, the Jefferson's report the following.

1.   The Jeffersons received a refund of 1998 Virginia income taxes of $45. In 1998, the Jeffersons' itemized deductions amounted to $7,498. Their 1998 taxable income was $28,000.

2.   George, is in the Ph.D. program. He received a "full" scholarship of $8,000. Tuition amounted to $5,000, while books and required supplies were $800. In addition George spent $1,800 traveling ($600 for public transportation, $500 for food, and $700 for lodging) to Washington, DC to use the SEC's library, $1,000 photocopying financial statements, $1,000 to hire a statistical consultant, and $300 to hire an editor. These expenses related to George's research work for his Ph.D. dissertation.

3.   During the year, Martha's parents made several cash gifts to the Jeffersons. The gifts were invested in a First National Bank money market accounts which generated $650 of interest income to George and Martha; interest income to Sarah of $4,000; and Emily received $3,500 in interest income.

4.   The Jeffersons support the Presidential Election Campaign Fund.

5. During the year the following stock transactions were made:

Stock	Date Acquired	Date Sold	Sales Price	Cost
ABC Corp.	12/30/87	5/31/99	$2,400	$1,200
JUNK Corp.	9/15/98	8/25/99	2,000	8,000

6. The Jeffersons incurred the following expenses during the year:

a.	Sales tax on the purchase of a new car	$ 400
b.	Cash charitable contributions (U of Virginia)	1,000
c.	Student loan interest	2,500
d.	Interest on home mortgage	3,300
e.	Safety Deposit Box rental (for securities)	50
f.	Tax return preparation fee	400
g.	Real estate taxes	700
h.	Personal property taxes (based upon value)	250

7. During the year, the Jeffersons made a charitable contribution of XYZ stock to the University of Virginia. George had purchased the stock May 2, 1981 for $100. On April 1 of the current tax year, the *Wall Street Journal* provided a market quote indicating the value was $1,500.

8. George and Martha strongly supports the women's athletic programs at the University of Virginia. In August of the current tax year, George donated $500 to the athletic department's "CavsR'us Club." Members of this club receive two tickets for women's basketball with seats at mid-court and a preferential parking space in Lot 22. The normal price for season tickets is $50 each. Parking in Lot 22 is not otherwise available on game day. Parking in other lots on game days is free.

9. To enable George to attend school, the Jeffersons hired Nanny Smith who lives at 333 Childress Lane in Monticello. Her SSN is 444-33-2222 and she was paid at a monthly rate of $350 to care for Sarah and Emily. The Jeffersons completed the appropriate wage tax forms. Their employer identification number is 23-4875789.

REQUIRED: Prepare and print the Federal income tax return for George and Martha Jefferson.

PROBLEM 8 Ronald Lump

Objective: Self-employed professional, office in home

Ronald Lump, 55, is an unmarried, self-employed medical doctor and resides at 2601 Pennsylvania Avenue, Washington D.C. 20001. His Social Security number is 387-12-3456. Ronald's wife died last year, but he continues to maintain a home for his blind 16 year-old dependent son Ronald, Jr., whose Social Security number is 387-12-3457.   Ronald's telephone number is 202-555-1234.

The relevant tax information given to you includes the following:

1.   Ronald uses the cash method of accounting in his business. His employer identification number is 33-1234567. Income and expenses pertaining to his business follow:

a.	Fees collected	$ 295,000
b.	Bad debt written off	2,000
c.	Legal and accounting services	2,500
d.	Qualifying business meals and entertainment	1,400
e.	Medical journals	800
f.	Office supplies	1,300
g.	Continuing education self-study courses	3,550
h.	Malpractice insurance	34,000
i.	Part-time secretary from "Kelly Girl"	10,000

2.   During the year, Ronald worked at City Hospital and University Hospital, both in Bethesda, Maryland. While he spent 30 to 35 hours per week working at the hospitals, Ronald was not provided with an office at either hospital.

Instead, Ronald used a bedroom in his house as his office, where he kept a computer, an answering machine, a copier, telephone, patient records, and medical books and journals. From the office, Ronald contacted other doctors and patients by phone. In addition, he often called hospitals to arrange admission for his own patients. He did all necessary to bill his patients in this office. He also spent time in his office reading medical books and journals, and preparing for patients; however, Ronald did not see any patients at his office. On average, Ronald spent 16 hours per week working in his home office during this year. Ronald did not use the office for any non-business purposes. His part-time secretary also worked in the home office.

Ronald has the following expenses relevant to determining a home office expense deduction:

a. The bedroom office represented approximately 20% of the total square footage of his house.
b. Total interest expense paid on his home mortgage was $17,000.
c. Ronald's annual utility bills for the residence were $2,800.
d. Property taxes on the house amounted to $2,100 for the year.
e. Ronald paid $210,000 for the house when he purchased it on January 1 of this year.
f. Ronald has a second telephone line that can only be answered in his office. The cost of this business phone was $480 for the year.

3. In March, Ronald purchased office furniture costing $8,000. Ronald wishes to maximize any deduction relating to this furniture that is available to him this year.

4. Ronald made timely estimated Federal income tax payments of $80,000 ($20,000 each quarter) during the year; the fourth quarter payment was made on January 15, 2000. He also made estimated income tax payments for a total of $3,200 to the Maryland and the District's Commissioners of Revenue. Ronald made the last quarter's payment to both jurisdictions on December 31, 1999. He wanted that tax deduction. Ronald made an additional payment of $345 when he filed his 1998 D.C. income tax return in April, 1999. Ronald paid $125 in additional income taxes for 1998 to Maryland when he filed in April, 1999.

5. Ronald received $1,000 in dividends on savings held in a D.C. Savings Bank time deposit. In addition, he received a $600 dividend from his mutual life insurance company on a policy that he owns on his life. Accordingly, the cash value of the policy increased $600. He paid premiums on the policy of $2,500 during the year.

6. Ronald received the final settlement on the life insurance policy held on the life of Mrs. Lump. He received a lump-sum of $100,000, plus the first payment of $5,500, a life-time annuity. The insurance company reported that $1,500 of this amount was interest.

7. Ronald's other tax-related transactions were:

a. Doctor fees incurred for Ronald, Jr., $5,000
b. Real estate taxes on land held as an investment in Haiti, $500
c. Ronald elects to support the Presidential Election Campaign Fund.

REQUIRED: Prepare and print Ronald Lump's Federal income tax return.

PROBLEM 9 John and Jane Elder

Objective: Semi-retired wages, investment income, retirement income

John and Jane Elder, who are both semi-retired, live at 1040 Lakeview Drive, Orlando, Florida 32801. Their telephone number is 904-555-4444. John, who is 65, enjoys working part-time in the clubhouse at the Gator Golf Club, while Jane, who is 66 and legally blind, works at a local music store, Thomas Piano Company, as a piano tuner. John's and Jane's Social Security numbers are 154-32-1234 and 265-43-2123, respectively. The information presented relates to their activities during the current tax year.

1.   From John's $15,000 salary earned at the Gator Golf Club, federal income taxes withheld were $1,200, Social Security taxes withheld were $930, and Medicare taxes withheld were $218.

2.   Jane's earnings totaled $13,000; withholding for federal income tax was $540; for Social security, $806; and for Medicare tax, $188.

3.   Other items of income received during the year included:

   a.   John's pension from his former employer was $4,800. All contributions to the pension fund were provided by Alcoa, his former employer.
   b.   Interest Income:
       i.   Best Money Market Fund, $850
       ii.   First Orlando Bank, $2,450
       iii.   Interest on a City of Miami general obligation bond, $600
       iv.   The Elders have no accounts in foreign banks.

4.   Other Income:

   a.   Dividends from Security Corporation stock, $3,000
   b.   Taxable pension proceeds from Security Corporation, $5,000
   c.   Jane received an annuity of $300 per month from the Rock Insurance Company. The proceeds were paid in accordance with a single premium annuity policy Jane had purchased 30 years ago for $12,000. 1999 is the second full year of the 10-year term certain annuity policy.

5.   As a result of a hurricane during September, the Elders' Volvo station wagon was totally destroyed. Its value at the time of destruction was $15,000, while its original cost was $22,000 when purchased on October 1, 1994. Unfortunately, the auto was not insured; John forgot to pay the bill.

6. Because of circulatory problems diagnosed during a routine physical examination, Jane's physician recommended that she begin a daily swimming routine. There are no pools available to the Elders. Consequently, the Elders had a swimming pool constructed in their backyard. While the cost of the pool was $15,000, it only increased the value of the home by $5,000.

7. Routine uninsured medical expenses included:

a.	Doctors	$500
b.	Prescription medicines	600
c.	Over-the-counter medications	150
d.	Medicare, part B	500

8. Other expenditures made during the year include:

a.	Gift to their son	$10,000
b.	Cash charitable contribution	4,500
c.	Tax return preparation fee	300

9. In the event a tax refund is due, the Elders would like one-half of it credited to their tax liability for next tax year. They both fully support the Presidential Election Campaign Fund.

REQUIRED: Prepare and print the Elders' Federal income tax return.

PROBLEM 10 Nancy and Steve Ferguson

Objective: Stock transactions, itemized deductions, tax refund

Nancy and Steve Ferguson, both 36, are married and live at 777 Millbrook Court, Charlotte, North Carolina 28203. Their telephone number is 704-444-5555. Nancy's Social Security number is 223-34-4556 and Steve's Social Security number is 277-88-9900.   They fully support the Presidential Election Campaign Fund.

1.   Nancy teaches home economics at Charlotte High School and earns an annual salary of $25,000. Federal income taxes withheld were $3,000, Social Security taxes withheld were $1,550, and Medicare taxes withheld were $362. State income taxes withheld were $1,500.

2.   Steve was employed at Millbrook Lumber Co., a lumber yard, as an inventory specialist. His W-2 showed a salary for the year of $28,000. From his earnings, Federal income taxes withheld were $3,500, Social Security taxes withheld were $1,736, and Medicare taxes withheld were $406. State income taxes withheld were $1,680.

3.   During the year, the Fergusons received a $600 refund because of an overpayment of their previous year's North Carolina income tax liability. Last year they itemized their deductions on their federal income tax return. (In 1998, Schedule A, Line 26 was $8,660 and taxable income was $40,700.)

4.   During the year the following transactions were executed:

Item	Date Acquired	Date Sold	Sales Price	Cost
Personal automobile	3/30/86	9/30/99	$ 3,000	$10,000
XYZ Stock	10/20/97	7/ 3/99	$23,000	$22,500
CDE Stock	1/ 3/81	12/31/99	$ 9,000	$ 6,000
FGH Stock	9/30/99	11/28/99	$ 1,000	$ 3,000

5.   On December 29, 1999, Nancy and Steve sold 1,000 shares of MNO Corp. stock to Nancy's brother. The sales price was $5,000. The MNO stock was originally purchased by the Fergusons for $7,500 on October 26, 1984. Because of their hope that the stock would rebound, Nancy repurchased the stock from her brother for $5,100 on January 8, 1999.

6.   Other tax related expenditures include the following:

      a.   Employee expenses for lodging incurred by Steve on a business trip -- reimbursed and included in Steve's W-2, $600

      b.   Contribution -- First Reformed Church, $1,500

      c.   Credit card and automobile loan interest, $600

      d.   Mortgage interest on personal residence, $4,000

      e.   Interest paid on home equity loan totaled $3,500

      f.   Property taxes on home, $1,780

REQUIRED: Prepare and print Nancy and Steve's Federal income tax return.

PROBLEM 11 Dick Craig

Objective: High income, divorced, sale of home, stock option

Dick Craig, 47, is the vice-president of Marketing for the St. Louis Beverage Company, One Main Street, St. Louis. He lives at 5414 Presidential Lane, St. Charles, Missouri 63301, and his telephone number is 314-555-5555. Dick's Social Security number is 477-22-5900. The information presented relates to his activities in 1999.

1.   Dick's salary was $175,000. Federal income taxes withheld were $45,000, state income taxes were $10,800, Social security taxes were $3,887, and Medicare taxes were $1,958.

2.   Interest income from Bank of St. Charles, $2,000

3.   Dividends on St. Louis Beverage stock, $12,000

4.   In 1997, Dick and his wife Esther were divorced. The divorce decree awarded custody of their son, Bob, to Esther and provides that Esther is to receive $400 per month for child support. The decree further stipulates that Dick was to pay $140,000 of alimony in 1997, $80,000 of alimony in 1998, and $4,000 per month as alimony for 1999 and later years. Dick paid the alimony and child support as required by the divorce decree. Esther's social security number is 555-55-5555.

5.   The divorce decree also required that Dick and Esther's home be sold and the proceeds divided equally between them. Dick handled the sale. On January 10 of the current tax year, the house was sold for $250,000. The joint basis in the house was $180,000. Real estate commissions of $13,500 were paid on the sale. The existing mortgage on the house had a balance of $120,000, which Dick paid off. The balance of the proceeds was distributed equally to Dick and Esther on January 15.

6.   On March 15, Dick purchased his current home. The cost was $150,000. Dick paid $15,000 down and obtained a mortgage of $135,000 from the Bank of St. Charles. He was able to obtain an interest rate on the mortgage of 6% by paying 1 point ($1,350), which is the standard practice in the area. During the current tax year, Dick paid $6,100 interest on the mortgage in addition to the 1 point.

7.   On July 1, as a result of his annual performance evaluation, Dick was granted an option to purchase 10,000 shares of St. Louis Beverage stock for $50 per share, the then market value. Dick agreed to purchase the shares. He borrowed the entire amount from the St. Charles Bank. (His brother is president of the bank.) During the remainder of the year, he paid $20,000 in interest on the loan.

8.   Dick fully supports the Presidential Election Campaign Fund. In addition, Dick contributed $500 to the Committee to Reelect Senator Scandal.

9.   Dick received a refund of state income taxes in the amount of $386.   On his last year's tax return,   Dick had itemized deductions of $15,000 and taxable income of $105,000.

10.   Additional expenditures incurred during the current year were:

        a.   Cash contribution to U of Missouri, $1,500
        b.   Property taxes on his home, $3,500
        c.   Interest on car loan, $2,800

11.   Dick has no interest in any foreign accounts.

REQUIRED: Prepare and print Dick's Federal income tax return.

PROBLEM 12 Louise and Ernie Hansen

Objective: High income, self-employed taxpayer with an AMT problem

Louise and Ernie Hansen left the hassles of big city life to move to the small town that the world has forgotten and that has no telephones anywhere in town. They currently live at 52 Lake Rd., Lake Wobegon, Minnesota 55457.   Louise's Social Security number is 257-15-1122 and Ernie's is 075-22-1993. Ernie is the author of a series of self-improvement books. His latest is *How to better organize your office*. His publisher is sure it will be a best seller.   Louise and Ernie report the following potentially useful information for their current year tax computation.

1.   Ernie received royalties of $5,400 this year -- not a good year for self-improvement books.

2.   Ernie received $75,000 from Minnesota Investment Fund, a specialized mutual fund that invests only in State of Minnesota municipal bonds. The distribution was entirely from interest. The fund did not sell any of its bonds during the year.

3.   Louise inherited $200,000 cash from her father's estate. She used part of the funds to fix up the house and put the remainder in certificates of deposit at the Bank of Lake Wobegon. She received interest income of $5,600.

4.   In February, Ernie and Louise finally settled a long tax dispute with the State of New York. As a result, Ernie paid $39,000 in back taxes and $5,000 in interest.   In addition, he had to pay New York $4,000 in penalties.

5.   March 19 was Louise's lucky day. She won the Lake Wobegon lottery. As a result she received the first of twenty $75,000 annual payments. State taxes withheld amounted to $6,000. Federal income taxes of $21,000 were withheld. No Social Security or Medicare taxes were withheld.

6.   On December 1, Ernie cashed some of Louise's CDs and borrowed more to purchased a small, newly constructed shopping center in Lake Wobegon. He got it at a good price. The cost of the building was $550,000 and the land cost $75,000. Ernie decided to have the parking lot paved, at a cost of $50,000. Interest on the mortgage for the part year was $8,500. He held the shopping center in his own name. While he advertised for tenants in December, the first tenant did not move in until January 2, 2000; thus, he had no income from the property during the current tax year (1999).

7.   The Hansens fully support the Presidential Election Campaign Fund.

8.   Additional expenditures incurred during the current year were:

    a.   Cash contribution to St. Cloud State University, $3,500
    b.   Property taxes on their home, $2,500
    c.   Interest on car loan, $1,800

9.   It was a balmy day in May, three years ago, when the Hansens moved to Lake Wobegon. Among the several things they forgot, was to begin paying estimated taxes. They have been consistent ever since. Thus, no estimated taxes were paid for the current year's taxes.

10.   Concerned about his retirement years, Ernie decided to invest for the future. Accordingly, in June, he opened an IRA account at the local office of Oats Last, an investment brokerage firm. He contributed $2,000 to his account and $2,000 to an account for Louise. The funds were invested in equity stocks. At the end of the year, Ernie's account was valued at $1,900; Louise's was valued at $2,300. He should have invested in the same stocks as Louise.

REQUIRED: Prepare and print the Hansen's Federal income tax return.

PROBLEM 13 Bill and June Barber

Objective: Investment activities

Bill and June Barber live in a small town, Leroy, North Dakota. However, they are able to engage in a variety of investment activities from their town. They live at 1 Archer Lane, Leroy, ND 58252. Their telephone number is 701-555-5555. Bill's Social Security number is 254-35-7622 and June's is 475-32-1286. The tax events of 1999 for Bill and June are listed below.

1.   Bill received interest from the Bank of Leroy, of $12,400.

2.   June received the following dividends:

   a.   General Motors, $23,890
   b.   General Electric, $2,600
   c.   General Dynamics, $3,500
   d.   General Tire Company, $2,300
   e.   General Consulting Service, Inc., $345

3.   Bill purchased a tract of Texas farm land 30 years ago for $40,000. On January 5, it was worth $60,000. He exchanged it for farm land outside of Leroy (FMV $58,000). Later, on August 4, Bill sold one fourth of his Leroy land for $16,000, paying a sales commission of $1,600.

4.   Bill is a 50% owner in a limited partnership that owns a variety of real estate across the country. In prior years, the partnership reported several losses. As a result of the past losses, Bill has a passive activity loss carryover of $13,000. On August 4, Bill sold his entire interest in the partnership for $340,000. At the time of sale, his basis was $334,000. The partnership reported no income or loss for the current tax year.

5.   The Barbers paid estimated federal income taxes of $1,000 per quarter. In addition, they paid estimated state income taxes of $200 per quarter. Thinking ahead, the Barbers paid their fourth quarter payments in December of the current tax year.

6.   Ten years ago, Bill paid $240,000 for a tract of land he is holding as an investment outside of Dallas, Texas. The purchase price was comprised of $40,000 cash and a 20-year mortgage for $200,000 with a 12% rate. In October of this year, Bill was able to refinance the mortgage obtaining a new rate of 7%, and a new term of 10 years. To refinance the mortgage, he had to pay $1,000 in closing costs plus $2,000 in points. These charges were the normal fees in the area. The total amount paid as interest (excluding the points) for the year was $18,000.

7.   The Barbers fully support the Presidential Election Campaign Fund.

8.   Additional expenditures incurred during the current year were:

      a.   Cash contribution to University of Tennessee, $2,400
      b.   Bank mortgage interest on their home, $6,890
      c.   Property taxes on their home, $1,200
      d.   Interest on car loan, $800

REQUIRED: Prepare and print the Barbers' Federal income tax return.

PROBLEM 14 Roger and Barbara Holly

Objective: Small business with like-kind exchanges

Roger Holly, social security number 423-98-9876, operates an electrical contractor company at 111 French Avenue, Fries, Virginia 243301. The company has been expanding each year for the past several years. Currently, the company has five employees. Barbara Holly works in her home as a homemaker and as a part-time bookkeeper for the company.

Barbara's social security number is 422-45-6912 and they live on Route 3, Box 45, Fries, VA 24330. Their telephone number is 540-555-5454. They have two children. Bill is ten and his social security number is 456-23-7865. Matthew is seven and his SSN is 458-54-2389. Neither child had any income.

Both Roger and Barbara support the Presidential Election Campaign Fund.

Information about the business and their other tax transactions is listed below:

1.   Estimated federal income tax paid for the current tax year are $12,000; estimated state income tax paid during the current tax year are $2,500. In addition, they paid additional state income taxes relating to the previous year's income of $125 in April of the current tax year.

2.   Interest income from the Bank of Fries, $655

3.   Rental income from a small four unit apartment house that Barbara owns was $17,400. Barbara purchased the apartment house on February 4 for $145,000 and immediately begin renting the apartments. The mortgage interest on the apartments for the current year is $13,500; insurance is $500; and property taxes are $650. Roger did all the repairs at no cost to Barbara. (The cost of materials for the repairs ($125) was included in the expenses of Roger's business.)

4.   The Hollys have no interest in any foreign accounts or trusts.

5.   Roger trades trucks as often as he can afford to in order to minimize repair costs. On June 5, he was able to trade two trucks for new trucks. The new trucks (trucks 5 and 6) cost him a total of $10,000 in addition to the trade-in. The fair market value of the trucks (5 and 6) are $23,000 in total. The trucks that were traded-in (trucks 3 and 4) were purchased on January 2, last tax year, for $10,000 each, a total of $20,000. The Section 179 deduction was not taken on the trucks 3 and 4. All trucks weighed over 6,000 pounds.

6. Other income and expense items relating to the business are as follows:

    a. Purchase of various small tools, $1,500
    b. Rent on office building, $8,400
    c. Gas, oil, insurance, and other truck expenses, $13,500
    d. Employee salaries, $104,000
    e. Office supplies, $1,200
    f. Taxes paid, $12,000
    g. Licenses and fees, $4,000
    h. Beginning inventory of materials was $4,500; purchases of materials amounted to $123,000; and ending inventory was $7,200.
    i. Legal and professional fees amounted to $2,500 of which $200 was for preparing the Holly's personal tax return.
    j. This year, Roger wants to use the Section 179 deductions to the extent he can.
    l. Revenues from the business amounted to $340,000.

7. Possible itemize deductions included the following:

    a. Real estate taxes, $600
    b. Personal property taxes on cars, $340
    c. Bank home mortgage interest, $8,700
    d. Interest on bank credit cards, $1,050
    e. Contributions to their church, $5,500
    f. Investment in an IRA account at the bank, $4,000: $2,000 in Roger's name and $2,000 in Barbara's name

REQUIRED: Complete the Holly's federal income tax return using TurboTax.

PROBLEM 15 Alan Myers

Objective: Foreign Moving Expenses, Foreign Earned Income, Itemized Deductions Decision making

Alan Myers, social security number 435-97-0423, is a petroleum engineer employed by Petro Consulting, Ltd., 654 Crescent Ave., Kuwait City, Kuwait. Petro Consulting's office in the United States is 7710 Alamo Lane, Dallas, Texas. Petro Consulting is a foreign entity. Alan's address in Kuwait is 11B Al Fahim Square, Al Ahmadi, Kuwait.

Alan is a single individual with no dependents. He moved to Kuwait on January 3. He remained there for most of the year, except for a brief trip back to the United States to visit his family, from July 1 to July 10. During the year, Alan was paid a salary of $75,500. In addition, he was given a home leave allowance of $3,000 so that he could visit his family in the United States. For the year, Alan had $6,500 of qualified housing expenses associated with his stay in Kuwait. Because there are no taxes in Kuwait, Alan wishes to take advantage of the foreign earned income exclusion. Assume that Alan's tax home is in Kuwait (he expects to remain employed by Petro Consulting in Kuwait for at least 2 more years.)

Additional information needed to complete Alan's tax return is provided below:

1.   Alan owns some unimproved real estate in Seal Rock, Oregon. The real estate taxes on the property for the year were $1,080.

2.   Alan gave two qualifying cash charitable contributions during the year -- $1,800 to University of Colorado, and $2,000 to Amnesty International, a US corporation qualifying under IRC 502(c)(3).

3.   Alan paid $2,400 for medical insurance. In addition, he paid $200 for eyeglasses, $150 for dental checkups, and had $600 of other medical expenses -- none of these expenses were reimbursed by his insurance.

4.   Alan paid $50 for a safe deposit box, $400 for tax preparation, $300 for professional dues and journals, and $500 for unreimbursed employee business expenses (for a firefighting suit made of Kevlar and asbestos.)

5.   Alan incurred several expenses related to his move to Kuwait in January. Information related to the move is provided below:

    a.   Cost of moving his personal effects and household goods was $6,000.
    b.   Cost of travel to Kuwait: $875 airfare and $80 for meals.
    c.   For the first 14 days that Alan was in Kuwait, he stayed at a hotel (costing $70 per night), while he searched for permanent housing. During his hotel stay, the cost of his meals was $392.
    d.   Before moving to Kuwait, Alan was employed as a petroleum engineer in Houston, Texas.

6.   Alan does not support the Presidential Election Campaign Fund. The only foreign financial accounts he has is his checking account at the Bank of Kuwait. The average balance in that account was $1,000.   The highest balance was just after receiving his paycheck and was $3,200.

REQUIRED: Complete Alan's federal income tax return using TurboTax

PROBLEM 16 Terry Arnold

Objective: Gross Income transactions, Net Operating Loss

Terry Arnold, SSN 231-23-1231, is a single taxpayer. She began work as a self-employed graphics designer in June. Terry lives at Rt. 1 Box 421, Lawn, PA 17041.

The following tax related events occurred during the year:

1. Terry won a TV set in a raffle held to benefit the high school band. The TV set cost the band $350. The set had a list price of $585, but was recently on sale for $455.

2. Terry has 500 shares of Bankadoo stock. A $1 per share dividend was declared December 15, 1999, which was payable January 15, 2000.

3. On January 5, 1999, Terry cashed a check from the state lottery for $2,500, which had arrived in the mail at her residence during the last week of 1998. Terry was on vacation and did not find the check until she returned on January 2, 1999.

4. Terry paid $9,000 in mortgage interest during the year on her home. In addition, she paid $1,070 in property taxes on her house and made a charitable contribution of $875 to her church.

5. To help finance her new graphics design business, Terry sold 5,000 shares of ZenCo stock. She had purchased the stock on July 1, 1991 for $32,000. The sales price of the stock on the date of sale, April 5, 1999, was $30,000.

6. Terry had $80,000 of gross receipts from her new business, Terry's Graphics Design. She also had the following expenses:

    a. Advertising, $4,500
    b. Office Rent, $6,400
    c. Computer Rental, $3,000
    d. Business License, $500
    e. Utilities, $1,200
    f. Office Supplies, $500
    g. Accounting/Legal Fees, $300
    h. Wages paid to part-time help $1,000

7. Terry does not support the presidential election campaign fund nor does she have any foreign financial accounts.

8. Prior to June, Terry was a student at the University of Lawn. During the spring semester, she received a graduate assistantship that required her to be a full-time student and to work in the college 10 hours per week. She received $2,500. She paid tuition of $1,800 and purchased $300 in books. The balance was used for food.

REQUIRED: Complete Terry's federal income tax return using TurboTax.

PROBLEM 17 Stuart Dent

Objective: Gross Income transactions, Final return

During the year, Stuart Dent, SSN 229-22-9229, was enrolled as a full-time student at Texas Tech. His school address was 467 Nashville Road, Lubbock, TX 79409. Stu also worked part-time at the University Book Shoppe (employer number 12-6767676). He earned $2,242 with $139 withheld for Social security and $33, for Medicare taxes.

During breaks and summers, Stu worked as a waiter at Mom's Home Cookin'. During the summer, he earned $800 in wages and $560 in tips. Social security taxes withheld amounted to $84 and Medicare taxes were $20. No federal income tax was withheld.

Stu received a $2,000 scholarship to help defray the costs of college. Stu's college expenses for the year included the following:

Tuition	$1,500
Books	$425
Food	$2,500
Lodging	$1,800

Stu paid $500 in estimated quarterly federal income tax payments, $125 at each payment date.

Several years ago, Stu received an inheritance from his grandmother consisting of several financial securities. Income from these investments are as follows:

1.   Interest on State of Texas Bonds: $2,300
2.   Interest on US Treasury bonds: $4,050
3.   Dividend income:

   a.   General Motors, $436
   b.   IBM, $642
   c.   AT&T announced a 2 for 1 stock split for date of record of July 10. Stu held 400 shares valued at $40 per share. His adjusted basis in the stock was $10,000.
   d.   Apple Corp. distributed a 2% stock dividend, on September 15. This resulted in Stu receiving an extra 14 shares of stock when the value of the stock was $23 per share.

4.   On December 28, Stu was on his way to Dallas to attend the Cotton Bowl. Stu was in a traffic accident, he fell asleep at the wheel. Unfortunately, Stu was dead on arrival at the Dallas hospital. The car was valued at $12,000 just before the accident. Stu's car was totally destroyed. The car insurance proceeds of $10,000, were assigned to the bank to settle the outstanding loan on the car of $8,000.

5.   On December 29, Stu's paycheck for working at Mom's Home Cookin' came in the mail. The gross amount of the check was $300 with federal income taxes of $50, Social security taxes of $23 and Medicare taxes of $4 withheld. Stu's father cashed the check and used the proceeds for funeral expenses.

6.   On December 30, Stu's father was going through some of Stu's things when he found a coupon bond registered in Stu's name. Father clipped the attached coupon and took it to the bank. The bank credited father's account for $135, the interest for the six months ending December 1.

Due to his financial independence, Stu's parents do not claim him as a dependent. Stu supported the political process and the presidential campaign fund. Stu will take the standard deduction.

REQUIRED: Complete the Stu's federal income tax return using TurboTax.
You may need to perform some tax research to complete Stu's return.

PROBLEM 18 John Fauchon

Objective: Small business transactions and estimated tax

John Fauchon is a self-employed painter. His social security number is 261-16-1261 and his address is 231 Main St., Chicago, IL 60666, and his telephone is 312-555-5544. John is single and operates Fauchon Painting out of his rented home. He uses the second bedroom as his office. The bedroom is 500 square feet. His home has a total area of 2,000 square feet. John's rent for his house is $250 per month ($3,000 per year) and his total utility costs for the year were $1,600.

John grossed $142,000 in his business during the year. He operates under the cash method of accounting and has essentially no inventory at year end. The costs of materials and outside labor amounted to $44,000. In addition he incurred the following expenses:

1.   Advertising costs were $1,200
2.   Insurance costs were $2,300
3.   Legal and accounting costs were $500
4.   A customer refuses to pay a $4,000 bill. John talked to his attorney and determined that taking the case to court would not be cost effective, so he is giving up on collecting the bill.
5.   John leases all of his equipment. His leasing costs for the year amounted to $5,700.
6.   John paid $3,600 during the year for his health insurance coverage. Fortunately, he was healthy the entire year and did not incur any medical expenses.
7.   His telephone bill for the year was $1,200 which included business related long distance calls of $400. The monthly charge for phone service was $60 per month. He estimate that 75% of his local calls were business calls.
8.   In addition to his home telephone, John purchased a cellular phone which he carries with him in his rented truck. The phone cost $150 and the phone charges for the year were $240. John estimates that 30 per cent of the calls on this phone are personal; 70%, business related.

John's income varies greatly. His taxable income last year was only $35,000. He had paid no estimated taxes for that year, thus in April of the current tax year, he paid $4,900 in federal income tax, $4,945 in self-employment taxes, and $1,800 in state income taxes when he filed his tax returns. On December 15, 1999, he paid $10,000 in estimated federal taxes. This was his only payment of the year. John does not want to contribute to the President Election Campaign Fund.

REQUIRED: Complete John's federal income tax return using TurboTax.

PROBLEM 19 George and Barbara Foley

Objectives: Property transactions and potential hobby loss

George and Barbara Foley are married with two children, Sam 4, and Ted 12. Social Security numbers are, respectively: 212-12-1212, 121-21-2121, 234-34-5345, and 222-33-4444. They live at 706 Caroline Street, Frederick, MD 21701. Child care for Sam was provided by Frederick's Playland, 80 South Street, Frederick, MD 21702, employer ID number 12-5675432, and cost $5,200 for the year. Ted was old enough to take care of himself, but not old enough to take care of Sam.

George works for the investment banking firm, Churnum & Burnum, employer number 12-23412334. His salary was $47,000 and withholdings were as follows: Social security, $2,914; Medicare taxes, $682; Federal income, $7,620; and state income, $1,200. George also made federal estimated tax payments of $1,000 per quarter as scheduled.

George's salary, in addition to investment income, allows Barbara to pursue her love of painting. This endeavor is not yet profitable, but Barbara reasons that most great artists are not recognized in their own time. She spent $1,200 on supplies and other expenses and sold 2 paintings for $400 each. Her federal tax ID number is 23-3456789.

The Foleys financial activities during the year include:

1.   They sold 400 shares of IBM on July 5, for $46 per share. 200 shares were purchased eight years ago on May 4, for $50 per share. Three years ago the stock made a 2 for 1 split, when the value of the stock was $60 per share.

2.   During the year, the Foleys moved across town, a total of 52 miles. Churum & Burnum wanted their employees to live in the best part of town. Their former home was 31 miles from George's place of employment, and their current home is 20 miles from George's work. George paid the moving company $1,500 for the move. His employer gave George a moving grant of $1,000 which was **not** reported on his W-2.

3.   George and Barbara sold their former house for $80,000. The house had an adjusted basis of $60,000.   They purchased their current residence for $100,000 two months after selling the old one.   Both houses qualify as principal residences.

4.   On July 5, the Foleys sold 200 shares of APCO stock for $5,000. The original cost of the stock was $3,000 when it was purchased exactly three years earlier. Also on July 5, they purchased 100 shares of Consolidated Edison stock, also for $5,000. Both stocks are utility companies with equivalent risks and returns.

5. On October 12, Barbara paid Arthur & Price, CPAs, $1,500 for preparing a cash projection and business plan for an art gallery to be located in Frederick. Barbara decided not to go into the business at this time, but perhaps later. A&P advised her that now was not the best time to start a new business.

6. George is concerned about the high cost of college tuition (so is everyone else.) Accordingly he invested $1,000 in the Growth Mutual Fund in Sam's name and $3,000 in Ted's name to the same fund. George retained the right to sell the shares for the boys' benefit. The Growth Fund reported dividends of $30 and long-term capital gains of $100 to Sam; dividends of $90 and long-term capital gain of $300 to Ted. This is the only income received by Sam and Ted during the year.

7. George and Barbara do not support the presidential election campaign fund.

REQUIRED: Complete the Foley federal income tax return using TurboTax.

$200 \times 50 = 10,000$

$200 \times 60 => 400 \times \$30$

421200

PROBLEM 20 Carol Gatti

Objective: Small Business Return

Carol Gatti, social security number 612-21-4567, rents a house at 613 Indiantown Road, Hasty, CO 81044. Carol's telephone number is 719-555-7654. She is single and operates a sole proprietorship selling computer equipment. Carol incurred the following transactions relating to her business and other tax-related activities during the year:

1.   Office equipment costing $12,000, purchased in November and a delivery van costing $10,000 was purchased on June 1. She decided to elect Section 179 treatment.

2.   Because she feels image is very important in this business, she bought a BMW 325i for $33,000 on September 1. It was used 90% for business.

3.   Last year on January 1, $2,000 of office furniture was purchased. She did not elect Section 179 with regard to this asset.

4.   Revenues from the business totaled $200,000.

5.   Other information relating to their business is listed below:

   a.   Advertising , $3,000
   b.   Delivery van expenses, $2,000; BMW operating expenses, $4,000
   c.   Accounting, $1,500
   d.   Supplies, $800
   e.   Utilities, $1,800
   f.   Beginning inventory, $35,000; Purchases, $125,000; and ending inventory, $40,000
   g.   Store rent, $16,000

6.   Carol contributed $3,500 to a retirement plan organized under the Keogh plan provisions. The money was deposited on September 2.

7.   Carol paid estimated federal income taxes of $30,000; estimated state income tax of $4,000. All of these taxes were paid during the current tax year.

8.   Carol supports the Presidential Campaign Fund.

REQUIRED: Complete Carol Gatti's federal income tax return using TurboTax.

PROBLEM 21 Anthony Singlterry

Objectives: Investments and alimony

Anthony Singlterry, social security number 231-47-9748, is currently single with no dependents. He lives at 34 Hernrico Lane, Reading MA, 01867. His telephone number is 508-555-8765. Anthony works at United Parcel Service as a driver and makes $44,656 a year. Social security tax withheld was $2,769; Medicare tax, $646; Federal income taxes, $5,434, and state income tax, $1,409.

Ten years ago, Tony divorced his wife. The divorce agreement provided that he would pay alimony of $12,000 per year. In the current year, he paid his ex-wife $6,000 in cash and gave her stock in Apex Machine Corporation that was worth $6,000 on August 15, the day he transferred it to her. The stock had cost him $2,000 when he purchased it in August, 1989. She sold the stock on November 12, for $4,000. Tony's ex-wife's SSN is 521-86-9534.

Three years ago, Tony bought five $1000 Exxon corporate bonds at their face value. Due to the recent decline in interest rates the bonds are now selling at 108. Tony thinks that interest rates will climb in the near future, so he sold the bonds on July 8 for their current price, 108. Tony received $450 interest from the bonds during the year.

Tony also purchased some stock in a military defense startup company, HiTech Avionics, in late December, 1998, for $5,000. Unfortunately, the contract for a new missile guidance system that the firm was banking on was canceled due to cuts in the defense budget. The announcement came just 11 days later, on January 5, 1999. By the next day the stock was deemed totally worthless. He still held the stock at the end of the year.

Other stock transactions for the year included:

   1.   Stock in CAM Computer Corporation purchased on June 8, 1989 for $1,200 was sold on May 9 of this year for $5,000.

   2.   Stock in Lare BioTech which was purchased on November 7, 1998 for $5,400 was sold, at a loss, on May 7, 1999, for $1,500.

Tony supports the Presidential Campaign Fund and has no interest in any foreign accounts.

REQUIRED: Complete Tony's federal income tax return using TurboTax.

PROBLEM 22 Lewis and Vivian Willis

Objectives: Itemized deductions with casualty loss, charitable contributions

Lewis Willis (age 60) and his wife Vivian (60) live at 593 Depot Street, Indianapolis, IN 46291. Their social security numbers are, respectively, 423-54-7545 and 123-65-9345. They support the Presidential Elections Campaign Fund and may be reached at 317-555-5555.

Lewis works for the city of Indianapolis as a property assessor, and his wife works for BMG CD club as an order processor. Lewis and Vivian's W-2 information is as follows:

	Lewis	Vivian
Wages	$26,215	$21,642
Social security	$ 1,625	$ 1,342
Medicare taxes	$ 380	$ 314
Federal income tax	$ 2,252	$ 1,923
State income tax	$ 1,143	$ 947

Lewis and Vivian also paid property taxes of $1,400, mortgage interest of $627, credit card interest of $411. Their tax return preparation fee was $200. They also had considerable medical expenses as follows: insurance premiums of $3,500, prescription medication of $470, nonprescription medication $200, vitamins $150, and they also paid deductibles to doctors and hospitals in the amount of $1,500.

During the year, while the Willises were at the hospital, their house was robbed of the following possessions:

1.   In March, Jewelry costing $3,000, which had a fair market value of $4,000, was taken. The insurance company reimbursed them the full market value of $4,000.

2.   In August, other items that were not insured, with a cost of $3,000, and a fair market value of $2,000, were stolen.

The property was never recovered, but the criminals were caught. The Willises were so impressed with the way the police handled the incident that they decided to donate $1,000 to the Silver Shield Foundation, a qualified charity that supports the widows and orphans of officers that are killed in the line of duty.

The BMG CD club established a program five years ago that allowed its employees to purchase excess inventory items, CDs, at a discounted price. Vivian took advantage of the opportunity to purchase 500 CDs at a price of $2 each two years ago. The CDs had a regular price of $12.50 each. Vivian donated the CDs to the Indiana Home for Teens in Evansville, a qualified charity on September 3 this year.

Lewis has to use his personal automobile in his job because the city does not have cars for use by the assessor's department. The city reimbursed Lewis at a rate of $.20 per mile.

Lewis submitted expense reports for 10,000 miles of traveling and received $2,000. In addition to these business miles, Lewis drove 20,000 personal miles during the year, of which 3,000 miles were for commuting. While he was away from the office, he incurred $500 in food costs for lunches. None of the lunches were reimbursed by the city.

For several years, Lewis has worked with the youth group at his church. During the current year, Lewis used his personal automobile to take the youth group on outings. He drove a total of 4,000 miles. The church did not reimburse him for the trips.

In early December, Lewis and Vivian traveled to Dallas to attend a national church meeting as a representative of their church. They spent a total of six days in Dallas. Five of those days they were in all day meetings. On the sixth day, they went to Six Flags. The total cost of the trip was $1,400. The church did not reimburse them.

REQUIRED: Complete the Willis federal income tax return using TurboTax.

PROBLEM 23 Christine Willard

Objectives: Contribution of property, vacation home, business loss

Christine Willard (age 40) is a widow whose husband died last year. She has two children Tommy and Susan ages 14 and 17. Christine has an unlisted telephone number. They all reside at 345 Lakeshore Drive, Florence KY 41022. The family's social security numbers are:

	SSN
Christine	435-41-5743
Thomas	376-43-1634
Susan	357-27-4536

Christine is a scientist at a local pharmaceutical firm. Her salary was $78,354 with the following amounts withheld from her salary:

Social security	$3,887
Medicare tax	$ 991
Federal	$9,876
State	$2,987

On May 3, Christine contributed stock in Computerland with a basis of $500 and a fair market value of $2,500 to Queen's Medical Research Fund, 111 Kailua, Honolulu, HI, a qualifying charity. The stock was purchased on June 14, 1986. Christine also had interest income of $6,000 from investments in corporate bonds.

Christine incurred $5,500 mortgage interest on her home, $975 real estate taxes, and interest on credit cards of $345.

Christine owns a condo on the beach at Myrtle Beach, SC. She used the condo five weeks this year for family vacations and trips. She rents the condo to other families the remainder of the year. During the current year, she rented the condo for a total of 10 weeks at $650 per week. The condo cost $100,000 when she purchased it after her husband died last year. (She used some of his life insurance money.) She paid the real estate firm $1,300 for managing the property. Since the condo was new last year, there were no repairs. Insurance on the property cost $1,200.

Additionally, Christine is working on developing a drug on her own that could help in the treatment of sickle cell anemia. In developing this drug, she incurred research and development costs of $60,000 this year and $50,000 last year. In response to positive publications, the Sickle Cell Anemia Foundation awarded her a grant of $3,000 to help in her research. Christine is hopeful of receiving a major grant of $2.1 million next year. Christine's federal employer ID number is 45-6789012.

Christine does not support the Presidential Election Campaign Fund.

REQUIRED: Complete Christine's federal income tax return using TurboTax.

PROBLEM 24 Douglas Clayton

Objectives: Employee Expenses, moving expenses

During the year, Douglas Clayton SSN 223-65-9686 and single, moved from Atlanta, Georgia, to 1504 Towne Ct., East Peru, ME 04229 in order to keep his position in his company, Big Biz, Inc., employer ID number 55-1234567. The company did not pay any of the costs of moving. His old home is 1,500 miles from his new job location and 30 miles from his old place of work. Doug incurred the following expenses in the move:

1. Moving personal belongings, $2,200
2. Travel to new residence, $1,400
3. Apartment hunting trips, $1,800

Doug's W-2 reports his salary as $45,750; social security tax, $2,836; Medicare taxes, $663; Federal income taxes, $10,850; and Maine income taxes, $2,400.

Doug Clayton is an account executive for BigBiz, Inc., a major industrial supplier. His job requires him to travel on occasion, but his employer does not reimburse him. The employer feels that his salary is sufficient to offset the expenses of his travel. Doug has adequate records for all of the items listed below:

1. Doug personally paid for two business trips during the year. The first trip to Des Moines, Iowa was spent entirely on business. Airfare cost $600, lodging cost $500, and meals and entertainment expenses were $325 for the one week stay.

2. The second trip was for five days in Las Vegas, Nevada. He arrived on Sunday evening and started with his business meetings on Monday morning. On Wednesday, he completed the negotiations and felt good about the week's work so far. The primary purpose of the trip was for business, but Doug finished business matters on Wednesday, and spent the last two days gambling. Hotel, meals and entertainment expenses were the same for each of the five days. The cost were Airfare, $625; lodging, $765; and meals and entertainment, $425.

3. Doug did reasonably well at the gaming tables in Vegas. The first day of gambling, he won $5,000. The second day he was not so lucky; he ended the day losing $3,000. Thus, he ended the trip with $2,000 profit from gambling.

Additionally, Doug drove his personal automobile 1,500 business miles. These miles were for trips around Maine on company business. On one occasion, he was late and drove a bit fast to make up the time. He got a speeding ticket that ended up costing him $250. His total miles driven were 25,000 including 2,500 commuting miles.

Doug's only other tax related transaction was his annual contribution to his alma mater, Georgia Tech. He gave $300 this year. He supports the Presidential Election Campaign Fund.

REQUIRED: Complete Doug's federal income tax return using TurboTax.

PROBLEM 25 Dennis and Pat Garnett

Objectives: Passive activities

Dennis and Pat Garnett live at 32 Wilshire Drive, Home, KS 66438. Their telephone number is 913-555-5645. Pat is a real estate assessor for New Realty Company, and makes $35,000 per year. Social security withholding was $2,170; Medicare taxes, $508; federal income tax, $3,342; and state income taxes, $1,000. Dennis stayed home to take care of their son, Johnny and look after the family's investments. Social security numbers are as follows: Dennis 213-54-7468, Pat 324-63-7143, and Johnny 132-77-6143.

Dennis materially participates in a rental real estate activity, The One (ID number, 11-2233445), which reported a loss of $15,000 for this year (they have sufficient basis to absorb the loss). Dennis was a limited partner in another real estate venture, called The Second (ID number 22-3344556), with a beginning of the year basis of $20,000 and a net loss of $25,000 for the year. Yet another of Dennis's limited partnership involving real estate, (you guessed it) The Third (ID number 98-7654321) generated a $10,000 gain.

During the year, the Garnetts agreed to an out-of-court settlement from which they received $20,000 in compensatory damages and $60,000 in punitive damages. The defendant was Billy Joe Bob Dupree, a local televangelist who made slanderous remarks about the Garnetts on his television program after the Garnett's partnership, The Third, refused to sell him some land near a lot Dupree already owned. It seems that without Garnett's lot Dupree will be unable to fulfill his dream of building the world's largest amusement park cathedral.

Other tax related transactions included the following:

1. Mortgage interest on their home was $4,600.
2. Mortgage interest on their mountain cabin was $3,900.
3. Medical bills paid in excess of insurance was $2,300.
4. Personal property taxes amounted to $235.
5. Real estate taxes amounted to $895.
6. Charitable contributions to his church $600.
7. Contribution of $1,000 to the Bobby Carter Fund, a fund set up at a local bank to help pay the expenses of a young man who broke his back while on his senior class beach trip. The family can not afford the $50,000 medical bill.   There is no relation between the Garnetts and the Carters.
8. To call attention to the need for green plants, Dennis dug up a small cottonwood tree from his back yard and planted it on the courthouse lawn. The tree had a value of $100. The tree was on his lot at the time he purchased the property. He estimates that the value of the tree at the time he purchased his house in 1990 was $10.
9. They fully support the Presidential Election Campaign Fund.

REQUIRED: Complete the Garnetts federal income tax return using TurboTax.

PROBLEM 26 Mike and Mary Older

Objective: Retired executive with investment income

Mike and Mary Older are a retired couple who live at 4982 Burruss Road, Tempe, Arizona 85287. Mike is retired from his position as Chief Financial Officer for Bombay Furniture Company. Mike's social security number is 389-76-5421; Mary's, 367-43-9764, and their telephone number is 602-555-6786. After discussing their financial affairs for some time, you have gathered the following information.

1.   Mike receives a yearly pension from Bombay of $45,000. The pension is a lifetime annuity on his life only which was funded entirely by his employer. Both Federal income taxes, of $12,000, and state income taxes, of $2,300, were withheld from the pension during the year.

2.   The Olders have invested in the Growth Mutual Fund for several years. In the current year, they received ordinary income distributions of $63,000 and capital gain distributions of $28,000 from the fund. No federal or state taxes were withheld.

3.   Other items of income received during the year included:

    1.   Mike's Social Security receipts were $23,600.
    2.   Interest Income received were as follows:

        a.   Bank of Arizona, $3,200 on checking account
        b.   Tempe Savings Bank, $4,450
        c.   The Olders have no other accounts, foreign or domestic.

4.   The Olders sold stock that Mike had received from Bombay under a non-qualified stock option plan. The stock was worth $250,000 at the time he received it in May, 1989. Mike sold the stock on December 4, 1999 for $342,000. He deposited the proceeds in his checking account while he considered what to do with the funds.

5.   Mike has always been a supporter of education. In the July, a friend asked Mike to teach a class at Arizona State in Controllership. He agreed to do so. The university paid him $5,300 for teaching the class. It also withheld Federal income taxes of $480, social security taxes of $329, Medicare taxes of $77, and Arizona income taxes of $318. The faculty were pleased with Mike's performance and has asked him to teach again next semester.

6.   Routine uninsured medical expenses included:

        a.   Doctors, $800
        b.   Prescription medicines, $400
        c.   Over-the-counter medications, $350

7.   Other expenditures made during the year include:

      a.   Gift to their son, $10,000
      b.   Cash contribution to Arizona State, $4,500
      c.   Tax return preparation fee, $600

REQUIRED:

1.   Use TurboTax to prepare and print the Olders' Federal income tax return. They fully support the Presidential Election Campaign Fund.

2.   Advise the Olders' about what to do with the proceeds from the sale of their stock. For your information, State of Arizona bonds have an interest rate of 4%; average corporate bond rate is 8%; bank account rates are 5%; and the high risk bond rate is 12%.

3.   Determine the marginal taxes on the income from teaching if Mike agrees to do so in the Spring. For this part, assume that Mike will invest the funds from Bombay in the bank and earn 5% on the funds for the year. Is this a wise strategy?

For these required items, consider simply modifying the data input and compute the new tax amount.

Problem 27 Bob and Sue Brown

Objective: S corporation earnings and potential AMT problems; Tax planning for AMT

Bob Brown is the owner of Brown Inc. a small manufacturing in Statesboro, Georgia that makes magnetic plastic strips that can be imprinted with businesses names and given to customers for their refrigerators. The business has been moderately successful the past few years. Since Bob considers his business to be a small business, he elected to be treated as a Small Business Corporation under Subchapter S of the IRC; hence Brown Inc is a S Corporation.

Bob and Sue live at 789 Fortin Ave, Statesboro, GA 30460-8141 and their telephone number is 912-555-7655. Bob's SSN is 443-76-1234 and Sue's is 454-78-8621. Brown Inc. taxpayer ID number is 77-9873621 and corporate headquarters are at 89 Martin Road in Statesboro; ZIP code 34060. Sue works at home caring for their two children Karen (age 10, SSN 245-76-8421) and Spence (age 7, SSN 265-66-3456,) and overseeing their home with its two acre garden named "Tara".

Bob's accountant prepared the Form 1120S and reported the following items on Bob's form K-1:

Line 1, Ordinary income (loss) from trade or business	($60,000)
Line 4a, Interest income	12,000
Line 4e, Long-term capital gain	50,000
Line 5, Net gain under Section 1231	18,000
Line 14a, Depreciation adjustment on property, after 1986	30,000
Line 14b, Adjusted gain or loss	8,000

In addition to the income and expenses from Brown Inc, Bob and Sue report the following items:

1. Sue purchased private activity bonds issued by the city of Statesboro in 1994. The interest from these bonds amounted to $10,000 for the current year.

2. Bob inherited a one-third interest in the family farm located outside of Florence, AL. The farm is operated as Brown Farms, Ltd., a limited partnership with Bob's brother Jim as the general partner and Bob and his sister Alma as limited partners. Bob's share of the farming profits this year is $20,000. According to the partnership agreement all expenses are allocated to the general partner, thus, there were no other items reported on the K-1 from Brown Farms, Ltd. Brown Farms, Ltd. tax ID is 55-3423126.

3. Bob received dividends of $26,000 from his portfolio of stock. He did not sale any of his stock during the year.

4. In 1998, Bob greatly overpaid his state income tax. His itemized deductions in 1998 amounted to $12,980; his 1998 federal tax was $13,000. As a result of the overpayment, Bob and Sue received a refund from the State of Georgia in 1999 of $5,000.

5. Bob and Sue's itemized deductions include the following:

a.	Local property tax on Tara	$4,300
b.	Georgia estimated income tax paid in 1999	9,000
c.	Mortgage interest, on loan used to purchase Tara	24,000
d.	Home Equity loan used to purchase auto	7,000
e.	Contribution to Georgia Southern University	8,000

REQUIRED:

1. Use TurboTax to prepare and print the Brown's Federal income tax return. They support the Presidential Campaign Fund.

2. Assume that the Brown's are considering some potential transactions that will be completed during 1999. Consider the impact on their federal income taxes of the following transactions. In other words, recompute the Brown's tax return assuming the following changes.

    a. Pay an additional $1,000 in estimated state income tax during the year.
    b. Make a charitable contribution of stock that has a basis of $5,000 and a FMV of $15,000. The stock would be contributed to Georgia Southern, their favorite charity.
    c. Sell some stock they own that would result in a $4,000 gain.
    d. Bob would like to know if there would be any advantage to him to have the corporation, Brown, Inc, elect the deduction under Section 179 on the $10,000 of qualifying equipment purchased during the year. The qualifying equipment is a personal computer, printer, and other computer equipment that he purchased on April 1. If the corporation elected Section 179, the corporation loss would increase by $6,500; depreciation for regular income tax would decrease by $3,500; AMT depreciation would decrease by $2,000; and Section 179 deduction would increase by $10,000 and would be reported on Line 8, of Bob's K-1 from the corporation.

        Modify Bob's tax return to account for these changes and print Form 1040.

PROBLEM 28   Pat and Wilma Oceanview

Objective: Comprehensive individual tax return

Pat and Wilma Oceanview live at 34 Ocean Street in picturesque Charleston, South Carolina, zip code 29409, and phone 803-555-6655.   Pat is the controller for Nations Paper Corporation, which is headquartered in Charleston.   Wilma (SSN 422-76-7392) owns and operates an advertising company that specializes in chemical and paper companies.   They have two children -- Jon, SSN 233-87-5642, age 10; and Nancy, SSN 244-77-5643, age 15.

Pat's (SSN 443-87-9876) salary is $100,000. He contributes to a flexible benefit plan through a salary reduction agreement under IRC 125 in the amount of $6,500 per year, thus his W-2 shows gross salary of $93,500. In addition, the W-2 reports federal withholding taxes of $23,800 for income tax; $3,887 for social security taxes; 1,356 for Medicare tax; and $3,400 for state income tax.

Pat also reports that he traveled substantially on company business. In total, Pat spent $12,400 on airfare, $6,500 on lodging, $4,000 on food, and $500 on incidentals. Pat also used his personal car for 7,000 miles of business travel (commuting travel was 3,000 miles and personal travel amounted to 12,000.) Pat elects to take the mileage allowance for his allowable business miles. Nations Paper gives Pat a travel allowance of $30,000 to cover all his travel expenses. Pat then must account to the IRS for his expenses. Pat has all appropriate documentation for the expenses listed above. Pat's company makes a contribution to a qualified pension plan for his benefit in the amount of $10,000 per year. Also, the company provides basic medical insurance for he and his family. Additional health insurance coverage is available at a cost of $2,000 per year which Pat decided to purchase as a part of the flexible benefit plan. The other expenses paid by that plan, $4,500, are for part-time child care services.

Because of Pat's travel he received frequent travel miles which allowed him to get four roundtrip tickets that have a value of $2,200. He used the tickets to take the family on vacation.

Wilma has been very successful with her advertising agency. She uses the cash basis of accounting for tax purposes, operates as a sole proprietor, and reports the following information:

1.	Revenue	440,000
2.	Wages and benefits paid	103,000
3.	Office rent and expenses	45,000
4.	Professional services	120,000
5.	Magazine expenses	8,000

In addition, Wilma purchased specialized computer equipment that cost $65,000 on January 5. She wants to maximize her depreciation deductions and elects to maximize her Section 179 deduction.

Because of her interest in the print media, Wilma is investigating starting a monthly magazine that will address the problems of the chemical industry. She spent $8,000 doing a feasibility survey and investigating publication facilities. As of the end of the year, she is still uncertain if the time is right. Maybe next year. Her bookkeeper recorded the expenses as magazine expenses, item 5 above.

Pat paid federal estimated taxes of $35,000 and state estimated income taxes of $3,000 during the year. Other investment transactions are listed below:

1. Pat received interest from the Metro Life Insurance Company of $3,500. This interest is from a life insurance policy he owned on his first wife Helda who died 10 years ago. Pat elected to leave the policy proceeds with the company.

2. Pat invested in a limited partnership that owns and leases pulp wood hauling trucks to paper companies throughout the southeast. This year, the partnership reports Pat's share of the loss as $55,000. The partnership is named Trucks or Us and has a tax ID number of 44-8623457. It is located in Charlotte, NC.

3. Wilma is an one-third partner in Charleston Land Company which develops apartment houses. Her K-1 reports her share of the partnership's loss as $15,000. The partnership's ID number is 67-8527358. She meets monthly with here partners to review the month's business and to plan future projects. The meetings last about 4 hours each month.

4. Pat owns 450 shares of the Tax Exempt Mutual Fund (ID number 44-9988776) that invests only in bonds issues by states and subdivisions thereof where the interest is entirely exempt from federal income taxes. The fund reported that each share received $10 of interest income, long-term loss on sale of bonds of $2 per share, and long-term gain on sale of bonds of $1 per share.

Pat and Wilma reported the following itemized deductions.

1. Local property taxes paid of $1,200
2. Contributions to The Citadel, a state university in Charleston, $3,000
3. Tax preparation fee of $600
4. Interest expense on home mortgage of $12,000
5. Investment advice from Churnum and Burnum Investors, $300
6. Tax advice from Arthur & Price, CPAs $800

In addition, Pat and Wilma had a fire on October 1, at their beachfront condo. The fire completely destroyed the condo and its contents. The condo had cost $75,000 12 years ago and was valued at $130,000 at the time of the fire. The contents had cost $23,000 and were valued at $15,000 at the time of the fire. Their insurance paid $120,000 for the condo and

$12,000 for the contents. They accepted the payment with regret. The related land was valued at $200,000 before the fire; it increased to $210,000 after the fire.

To make things worst, Pat was his fishing boat shortly after the fire when he turn the throttle the wrong way and crashed into the pier. The boat had cost $13,000 and was valued at $8,500 was completely destroyed. He did not have any insurance. Fortunately, Pat only suffered a server headache from the lecture Wilma gave him about the lack of insurance.

Prior to the fire, Pat and Wilma had rented their condo to summer vacationers. During the year prior to October 1, they had rented the condo for 13 weeks (91 days). In addition, they had used the condo for 30 days; the remainder of the time, the condo was not used. The mortgage interest on the condo amount to $4,000; property taxes were $800; repairs amounted to $500; insurance was $1,000; fees paid to rental agent was $1,000; and revenue from rental fees was $10,400.

They told you that they fully support the Presidential Election Campaign Fund and that they have no interest in foreign bank accounts.

REQUIRED: Prepare the Oceanview's federal income tax return.

PROBLEM 29 Bob and Sally Mickels

Objective: The purpose of this problem is to provide a comprehensive tax return problem that may be work in parts. Each part after the first may be added or deleted as your instructor wishes.

It was a story book marriage. Bob and Sally Mickels were married on a riverboat traveling down the Mississippi, on New Year's Eve, December 31, 1998. The weather was picture perfect as they said their vows. Since gambling is legal on the boat, and it was Bob and Sally's day, they tried their hand at roulette. Before the night of gambling was over, Bob had won $12,000 and Sally had won $21,000. They started gambling at 8 PM and stopped at 1 AM on January 1, 1999, when the honeymoon began. The riverboat recorded their winnings and gave them checks for their winnings less 20% withholding. Bob's check was for $9,600 (withholding for federal income tax was $2,400); Sally's check was for $16,800 (withholding for federal income tax was $4,200). What a wedding day indeed!

Bob and Sally live at 456 Easy Street, Memphis, TN 38150, telephone 901-555-6766.

Bob (SSN 432-43-2534) works as a weatherman for WBTV in Memphis, Tennessee. For the year, the station paid him a salary of $58,000 from which it withheld $14,400 for federal income tax; $3,596 in social security tax; and $841 in medicare tax. The station's federal ID number is 66-8573623 and address of record is 6677 Beale Street, Memphis, Tennessee 38152.

Sally (SSN 234-87-6523) Mickels is an advertising executive for Blue Moon Ads, Inc. in Memphis, Tennessee.   She received a base salary of $55,000 from which Blue Moon withheld $13,200 for federal income tax; $3,410 in social security tax; and $797.50 in medicare tax. Blue Moon's federal ID number is 68-4528536 and address of record is 5600 Beale Street, Memphis, Tennessee 38152. In addition, Sally received a bonus check for $14,000 on Friday, December 30, at 4:55 p.m. Sally and Bob had left town to attend the Sugar Bowl in New Orleans, and did not return to Memphis until Monday morning, January 2, 2000. Sally found the check and took it to the bank at noon on Monday. No taxes were withheld from the check.

Part A: Prepare a joint tax return for Bob and Sally Mickels assuming that they use the standard deduction. Both Bob and Sally fully supports the Presidential Election Campaign Fund.

Part B. The story of Bob and Sally continues.

On February 1, Bob formed the Bob Mickels Production Company, a sole proprietorship engaged in the production of television and radio commercials. As a new company, Bob Mickels Production Company has had a rough time getting established. Bob made a strong effort during February, March and April to meet all the right people. During that three month period, he had lunch with potential clients on fifty different occasions. Bob paid for all these lunches, a total cost of $1,000 of which Bob estimated his meals cost half, $500. From this effort, Bob gain three clients. Time for Plan B.

During the rest of the year, Bob hit the golf club. He joined the Memphis Country Club (initiation fee $2,500; monthly club fees of $50, a total of $400 paid during the year) and played golf frequently. He did not play well -- a source of embarrassment to him and his potential clients. So he took golfing lessons from the club pro at a cost of $500. It helped, he played better, made a better impression and got new clients for his production company. Bob incurred $600 in food purchases directly related to his business, and $400 in personal charges. In addition, on December 28, Bob paid the first six months of monthly dues for 2000, a total of $300.

For the eleven months of 1999, Bob Mickels Production Company billed clients for $120,000 in fees. However, as of December 31, Bob had only collected $56,000. When he returned to Memphis after the Sugar Bowl trip, he found checks for $15,000 in his Monday mail. The envelopes containing the checks were postmarked on December 31. In addition to the promotion expenses above, the company had wages expense of $15,000 for a secretary; rent on studio and office space of $33,000; payments to independent contractors for camera operators, video engineers, and others technical support people of $45,000; and rental of equipment of $25,000. The independent contractors work for various television stations in the Memphis area and did the work for Bob on a part-time basis.

Neither Bob's nor Sally's employer provides health insurance for its employees. To provide some protection, Bob joined the Farm Bureau (membership fee $10) and purchased health insurance from Blue Cross and Blue Shield that covered both Bob and Sally. He paid $300 per month for this health insurance.

To help pay the bills from the production company, Bob borrowed $80,000 from the National Bank of Memphis and paid $6,600 in interest.

Part B.   Prepare Bob and Sally's joint tax return considering the information in Part A and Part B.

Part C. And yet there is more about Bob and Sally.

In late February, Sally and Bob signed up for a seminar on a cruise boat focused on basic accounting and reporting for business. The seminar covers topics on both recording and using accounting information. The brochures says that the seminar is "designed for both business owners and managers of businesses." The cost of the seminar was $300 per person (both Bob and Sally paid); the cost of the cruise and related air fare was $1,800 per person, double occupancy. The cruise ship sailed from Miami, traveled around the Caribbean stopping at Puerto Rico and the U.S. Virgin Islands, and returned to Miami.

In March, Bob and Sally purchased their new home on Easy Street. They paid $22,000 as a down payment; assumed an outstanding mortgage of $70,000 with an interest rate of 8% on which they paid $4,300 in interest. To complete the purchase of the loan, they took out a personal loan (not a mortgage on the house) at the National Bank of Memphis for $30,000 with an interest rate of 7% on which they paid $1,600 in interest. They hope to pay the loan off next year and did not want to incur the costs related to obtaining a mortgage.

Other itemized expenses they incurred are as follows:

a. Cash contributions to their church, $2,000
b. Cash contribution to University of Memphis, $3,000
c. Sales taxes on new car, $350
d. Property taxes on their house, $800
e. Contribution to the Memphis Shelter Home of used furniture that cost $3,500 and had a FMV of $800 according to the Memphis Appraisal Company. Bob paid this company $35 for the appraisal. The shelter home is a 501(c)(3) corporation.

All was not rosy for Bob and Sally during the year. In November, Sally was caught in a sudden ice storm in Memphis (rare indeed) while driving home. As a result of the ice, Sally wrecked her car. The cost of the car had been $25,000. Its estimated value before the wreck was $16,000; its estimated value after the wreck, $10,000. The insurance settled the case and paid $3,000. Sally sold the car "as is" to a dealer for $9,500. She replaced the car with a car costing $19,500.

Part C. Prepare Bob and Sally's joint tax return considering the information in Parts A-C.

PROBLEM 30 Jim and Charlotte Lamewood

Objective: Home office, AMT items, Passive Losses and Contributions

Jim and Charlotte are dedicated school teachers who have been the backbone of the Monroe County, West Virginia school system for several years. The live in Possum Hollow on Route 4, Box 433, Bluefield, West Virginia 26506, and their telephone number is 304-555-6774. Over the years they have been able to invest in a variety of projects including coal mines, real estate ventures, and even the stock market.

Jim's SSN is 589-23-8641 and he is head librarian at Bluefield High School. His salary is $34,000 with federal income tax withholdings of $4,800; social security tax of $2,108; medicare tax of $493; and state income tax of $1,350. The school system also contributes to a qualified retirement system and provides full health insurance coverage.

Charlotte's SSN is 836-16-2648 and she teaches fifth grade at the Westside Middle School. Her salary is $33,000 with federal income tax withholding of $4,500; social security of $2,046; medicare tax of $479; and state income tax of $1,245. The school system also contributes to a qualified retirement system and provides full health insurance coverage.

Nearly 17 years ago, Jim inherited some money from his father which he invested in the Blue Hill Mining Partnership. Jim is the limited partner with a 40% share of profit and losses. Ben Blue is the general partner. Jim's basis in Blue Hill Mining at year-end was $10,000 and the partnership has no liabilities. Jim's K-1 reported the following:

Line 1, Ordinary income (loss) from trade or business activities $12,000
Line 15d Depletion (other than oil and gas)   62,000

Jim and Charlotte jointly own four real estate investments. They are listed below:

1.   250 acres of mountain land which they hope to sell to a ski lodge development that has been discussed for several years. The property taxes on the land are $2,500; mortgage interest on the outstanding mortgage on the land is $3,700; and they paid $50 for additional liability insurance on their home owners policy relating to land. In addition, Jim spent four days walking over the land looking it over and doing a little hunting while he was there. He spent $80 on gas on these trips.

2.   A four unit apartment building at 453 Hill Street, Bluefield. The apartments are rented. For the year, the total rent was $14,400. The apartment building was purchased in five years ago for $86,000. Mortgage interest amounted to $4,000 for the year. Property taxes were $3,400; utilities paid by the Lamewoods amounted to $500; repairs were $450; and insurance costs $750.

3.   A small rental house at 34 Mountain Lane, Bluefield. The house is rented for $3,000 a year. The house was purchased 12 years ago for $24,000. Mortgage interest was

$800; property taxes were $400; utilities paid by the Lamewoods amounted to $200; repairs were $650; and insurance costs $150.

4. A community shopping center at 1000 Mountainview Drive. The center has two large stores and eight smaller stores. They purchased the center on January 2 of the current tax year for $950,000. The contract allocated $150,000 to the land, $70,000 to the parking area improvements, $10,000 for the center's office equipment, and $720,000 for the buildings. The rental income for the year was $154,000. Expenses included repairs to the roof of $22,000; property taxes of $31,000; insurance of $4,000; utilities of $6,000; and interest on the mortgage of $76,000. The parking lot was in bad shape and had to be repaved during the year. The cost of repaving the lot was $25,000 and was done on May 3. The paving company suggested paving the lot every ten years. Jim also employs his sister Marylou to manage the center. He paid her $22,000 including benefits. Marylou is a very competent manager, thus Jim and Charlotte only spent four hours in December reviewing the year with Marylou.

Jim and Charlotte's stock transactions for the year were limited. They believe in the investment philosophy of buy low and hold long. Actually they had only two transactions. On April 4, they sold 2,000 shares of GEE for $45 per share. They had purchased the stock on August 5, 1988, for $40,000. They paid sales commission of $8,000. On December 3, they donated 1,000 shares of BDE stock to West Virginia University, their alma mater. The stock was listed on the New York Stock Exchange at $87 per share on that date. They had purchased the stock on July 8, 1983 for $17 per share.

Dividend income from their portfolio is $6,300.

Other transactions include:
   a. Home mortgage interest of $4,000
   b. Cash gift to their church $2,500
   c. Annual Cash gift to WVU, $1,000
   d. Property taxes on their home, $300
   e. Supplies purchased for use in teaching at school, $430

Jim and Charlotte have taken one bedroom and converted it to an office. The room is 15% of their total square footage of their home. They paid $65,000 for their home when purchased. Their utilities amounted to $1,500 per year; monthly telephone charges are $24 per month ($288 per year) and they estimated 40% of the calls relate to either school or their real estate investments; offices supplies cost $250 of which half related to school and half to their investments; and insurance on their home cost $300. Recall that the property taxes and mortgage interest are listed above.

Jim and Charlotte support the Presidential Election Campaign Fund and have no interest in any foreign accounts.

REQUIRED: Prepare Jim and Charlotte's federal income tax return.

INDEX

Software License Agreement and Limited Warranty
Desktop Personal Tax Products

IMPORTANT INFORMATION — Please Read

Do not use the Software (which term includes the product documentation) until you have carefully read this Agreement, which provides the terms and conditions for its use. Installing the Software indicates that you have read, understand and accept this Agreement. If you do not accept this Agreement and purchased the Software from a retail store, then return the Software and accompanying items to that store within 60 days of purchase with a dated receipt for a full refund. If you purchased the Software directly from Intuit, return it with the original packing slip within 60 days to Intuit Returns, 6060 Nancy Ridge Drive, Suite 100, San Diego, CA 92121-3290.

As used in this Agreement, the terms "you", "your" or "user" are synonymous, and refer to a user or registered user, as the case may be, of the Software. A "registered user" is a person who purchases the Software and registers their purchase of the Software with Intuit.

Read the ReadMe file before using the Software. It contains important terms governing the use of and information about the Software and Intuit's related services. In TurboTax, the ReadMe file can be accessed from within the TurboTax program group. In MacInTax, the Read Me First file will appear upon installation.

Permitted Uses and Restrictions on Use

You are granted a personal, non-exclusive license to use one copy of the Software and any final edition thereof only on a single computer and a single terminal. You may make one archival or backup copy of the Software for your own use. However, because the Software is protected by the copyright laws, it is illegal: to make additional copies or otherwise duplicate or permit the duplication of the Software by any other means (including electronic transmission); to give copies to another person; or, to modify, adapt, translate, rent, sublicense, loan, resell for profit, distribute, create derivative works based upon or network the Software or any part thereof. The Software also contains Intuit trade secrets, and you may not decompile or otherwise reverse engineer the Software.

You may <u>not</u> use the Software to prepare tax returns, schedules or worksheets on a professional basis (i.e., for a preparer's or other fee for tax preparation services). Notwithstanding anything in this Agreement, Intuit has no responsibility or liability for damages or claims relating to any use of the Software or the Services on a professional basis.

Electronic Filing Services and Other Intuit Services

If you choose to file your return electronically, your tax return will be transmitted by modem via the Internet to the Intuit Electronic Filing Center, where it will be converted to a standardized format and, then, transmitted to the applicable federal or state taxing authority (the "Services") while Intuit retains any records required by law. Telecommunications charges may apply. Intuit cannot guarantee that the taxing authority will accept your return due to circumstances beyond Intuit's control (e.g., incorrect user information, malfunction of the tax authority's system, etc.). Additionally, the telecommunications delivery systems used for the Intuit electronic filing services, such as the Internet, can be unpredictable in their performance and may, for example, impede access to the Intuit electronic filing service or the performance of the Services from time to time. You agree that Intuit is not in any way responsible for any such interference with your use of or access to the Services. Further, Intuit may at any time change or discontinue any aspect or feature of the Services including, but not limited to, its availability. The Software adheres to applicable IRS regulations/policy that limit the maximum number of electronically-filed federal returns to five.

Intuit uses a variety of methods (e.g., in-product, Internet, fax and phone) to provide technical and customer support in connection with the Software (which services are included in the capitalized term

"Services" as used below). The terms and conditions governing the offering of these services, some of which have fees chargeable to you, are announced by Intuit from time to time. Consult the Software's ReadMe file or Intuit's web site (www.Intuit.com/support) for the most up-to-date information relating to these services and any associated charges, as well as updates to the Software.

Satisfaction Guaranteed

If you are not 100% satisfied with this Software, Intuit's entire liability and your exclusive remedy shall be to remove the Software from your computer and return it within 60 days of purchase to the store where you purchased it with a dated receipt for a full refund. If the store is unable to issue a refund, or you purchased the Software directly from Intuit, then return the Software with a dated receipt or packing slip within such 60-day period to Intuit Returns, 6060 Nancy Ridge Drive, Suite 100, San Diego, CA 92121-3290.

Limited Warranty

If the disks are defective, then return the Software to Intuit Returns, 6060 Nancy Ridge Drive, Suite 100, San Diego, CA 92121-3290 within 60 days of purchase with a dated receipt, and replacement disks will be mailed to you.

Intuit warrants to its **registered users** the accuracy of the calculations on every form prepared using the final version of the Software (i.e., includes all available updates). If you pay an IRS or state penalty and/or interest solely because of a calculation error on a form prepared using the final version of the Software and not as a result of, among other things, your failure to enter all required information accurately, your willful or fraudulent omission or inclusion of information on your tax return, your misclassification of information on your tax return, or your failure to file an amended return to avoid or reduce your penalty/interest after Intuit announced updates or corrections to the Software in time for you to file an amended return, then Intuit will pay to you the amount of the IRS or state penalty and/or interest paid by you to the IRS or state. In order for Intuit to notify you of updates or corrections to the Software, **you must register the Software**. In this regard, you are responsible for keeping Intuit apprised promptly of any change in your email address, mailing address and/or phone number so that you can be notified of such updates or corrections. If you believe such a calculation error occurred, please notify Intuit in writing at Intuit Inc., Tax Analyst, P.O. Box 28862, Tucson, AZ 85726-8862 as soon as you learn of the mistake (and in no event later than 30 days after the penalty is assessed). You must include a copy of the IRS/state notice, a copy of the applicable hardcopy tax return and a diskette with the applicable tax return data file on it. You are responsible for paying any additional tax liability you may owe and providing any other information Intuit reasonably requests.

DISCLAIMER OF WARRANTIES

Except as expressly provided above, this Software and the Services are provided "as-is" and, to the maximum extent permitted by applicable law, Intuit and its suppliers disclaim all warranties, express or implied, regarding the Software or Services, disk and related materials, including their fitness for a particular purpose, their quality, their merchantability, or their non-infringement. Intuit does not warrant that the Software or Services are free from bugs, interruption, errors, or other program limitations. Some states do not allow the exclusion of implied warranties, so the above exclusions may not apply to you. In that event, any implied warranties are limited in duration to 60 days from the date of purchase of the Software. However, some states do not allow limitations on how long an implied warranty lasts, so the above limitation may not apply to you. This warranty gives you specific legal rights, and you may have other rights that vary from state to state.

Tax laws and regulations change frequently and their application can vary widely based upon the specific facts and circumstances involved. Users are encouraged to consult with their own professional tax advisors concerning their specific tax circumstances. Intuit disclaims any responsibility for the accuracy or adequacy of any positions taken by users in their tax returns.

All warranties or guarantees given or made by Intuit with respect to the Software or Services (1) are for the benefit of the original purchaser/licensee of the Software only and are not transferable, and (2) shall be null and void if a purchaser/licensee breaches any terms or conditions of this Agreement. Intuit is not responsible for the performance of services or products offered by third parties in connection with the marketing and distribution of the Software.

LIMITATION OF LIABILITY AND DAMAGES

Except to the extent of the above warranty of calculation accuracy, the entire liability of Intuit and its representatives for any reason shall be limited to the amount paid by the customer for the Software or Services, as applicable, purchased from Intuit or its authorized reseller. To the maximum extent permitted by applicable law, Intuit and its licensors, distributors, dealers or suppliers are not liable for any indirect, special, incidental, or consequential damages (including damages for loss of business, loss of profits or investment, or the like), whether based on breach of contract, breach of warranty, tort (including negligence), product liability or otherwise, even if Intuit or its representatives have been advised of the possibility of such damages and even if a remedy set forth herein is found to have failed of its essential purpose. Some states do not allow the limitation and/or exclusion of liability for incidental or consequential damages, so the above limitation or exclusion may not apply to you.

The limitations of damages or liability set forth in this Agreement are fundamental elements of the basis of the bargain between Intuit and you. You acknowledge and agree that Intuit would not be able to provide this product on an economic basis without such limitations.

Miscellaneous

This Agreement sets forth Intuit's and its representatives' entire liability and your exclusive remedy with respect to the Software and Services, and is a complete statement of the agreement between you and Intuit. Headings are included for convenience only, and shall not be considered in interpreting this Agreement. This Agreement does not limit any rights that Intuit may have under trade secret, copyright, patent or other laws. The agents, employees, distributors, and dealers of Intuit are not authorized to make modifications to this Agreement, or to make any additional representations, commitments, or warranties binding on Intuit. If any provision of this Agreement is invalid or unenforceable under applicable law, then it shall be, to that extent, deemed omitted and the remaining provisions will continue in full force and effect. The validity and performance of this Agreement shall be governed by California law (without reference to choice of law principles), and applicable federal law. This Agreement is deemed entered into at San Diego, California, and shall be construed as to its fair meaning and not strictly for or against either party.

Export Restrictions

Software containing (1) the electronic filing features; (2) the 128-bit web browser; (3) the online banking features; or (4) any other encryption-related features that are otherwise restricted under the Acts is defined as "Controlled Software" for the purpose set forth herein:

You acknowledge and agree that the Controlled Software is subject to restrictions and controls imposed by the Export Administration Act and the Export Administration Regulations ("the Acts"). You agree and certify that neither the Controlled Software nor any direct product thereof is being or will be acquired, shipped, transferred or exported, directly or indirectly outside the United States or Canada or will be used for any purpose prohibited by the Acts; provided, however, U.S. citizens and U.S. permanent resident aliens may travel to countries not prohibited by the Acts with the Controlled Software when it is installed on their personal computer and not otherwise used or transferred in violation of the Acts.

Software that does not contain (1) the electronic filing features; (2) the 128-bit web browser; (3) the online banking features; or (4) any other encryption-related features that are otherwise restricted under the Acts is defined as Other Software for the purpose set forth herein:

You acknowledge and agree that the Other Software may be subject to restrictions and controls imposed by the Export Administration Act and the Export Administration Regulations ("the Acts"). You agree and certify that neither the Other Software nor any direct product thereof is being or will be used for any purpose prohibited by the Acts. You agree and certify that you are not a citizen or permanent resident of the following countries: Cuba, Iran, Iraq, North Korea, Libya, Sudan or Syria.

U.S. Government Restricted Rights

This section applies to any acquisition of the Software by or for any unit or agency of the United States Government (the "Government"). The Software shall be classified as "commercial computer software", as that term is defined in the applicable provisions of the Federal Acquisition Regulation (the "FAR") and supplements thereto, including the Department of Defense (DoD) FAR Supplement (the "DFARS"). Licensor represents that the Software was developed entirely at private expense, that no part of the Software was first produced in the performance of a Government contract, and that no part of the Software is in the public domain.

If the Software is supplied for use by DoD, the Software is delivered subject to the terms of this license agreement and either (i) in accordance with DFARS 227.7202-1(a) and 227.7202-3(a), or (ii) with restricted rights in accordance with DFARS 252.227-7013(c)(1)(ii) (OCT 1988), as applicable.

If the Software is supplied for use by a Federal agency other than DoD, the Software is restricted computer software delivered subject to the terms of this license agreement and (i) FAR 12.212(a); (ii) FAR 52.227-19; or (iii) FAR 52.227-14(ALT III), as applicable.

If the Software is delivered to a distributor, reseller, integrator or other non-Governmental entity (the "Intermediary") for ultimate delivery to the Government, either directly or through other intermediaries: (1) the Intermediary shall obtain no rights in the Software except the right to deliver the Software to the Government under the terms provided herein; and (2) the Intermediary shall not alter or remove any proprietary rights legends placed on the Software by Licensor.